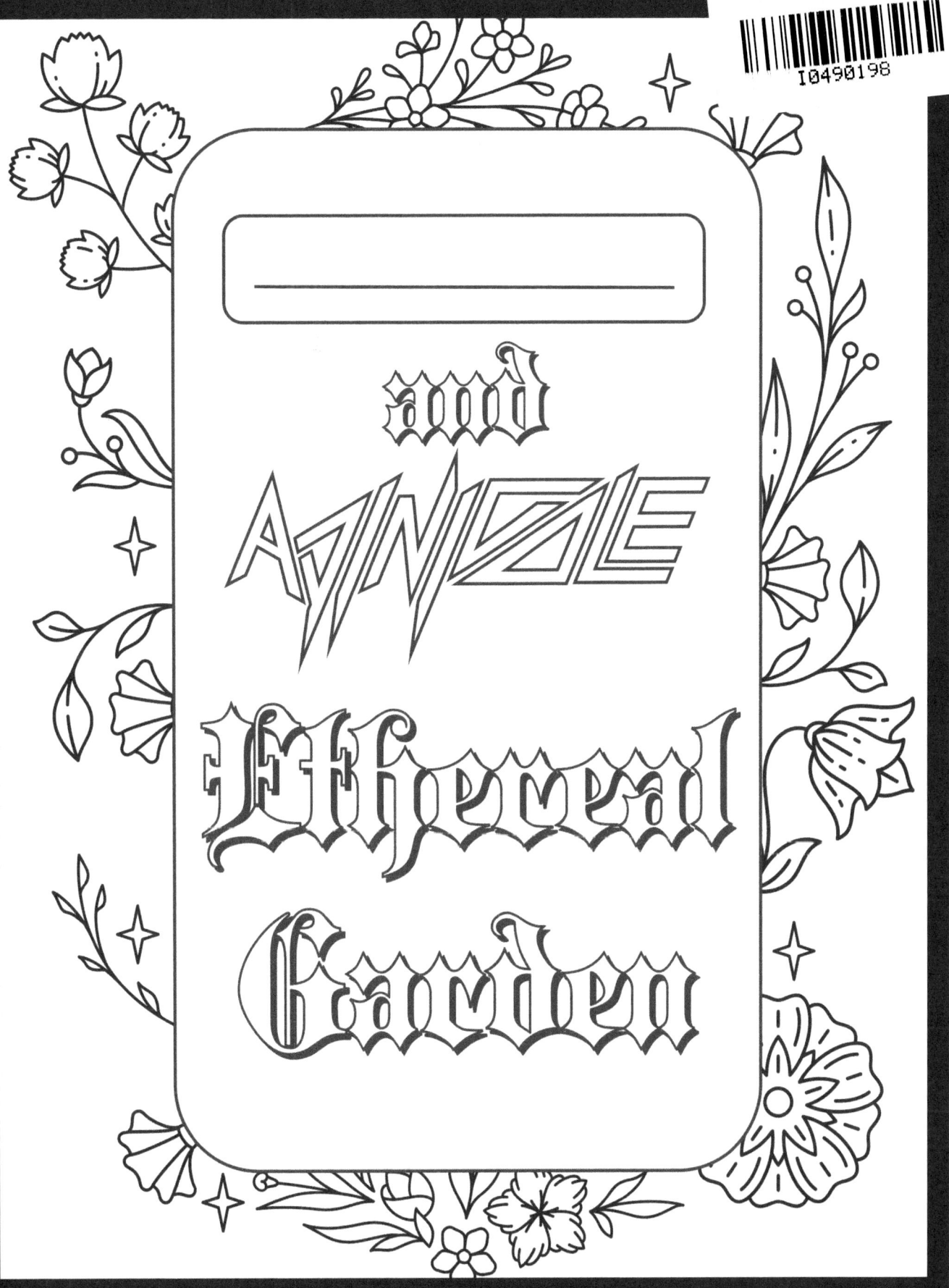

TAKE A SIP OF MY POTION

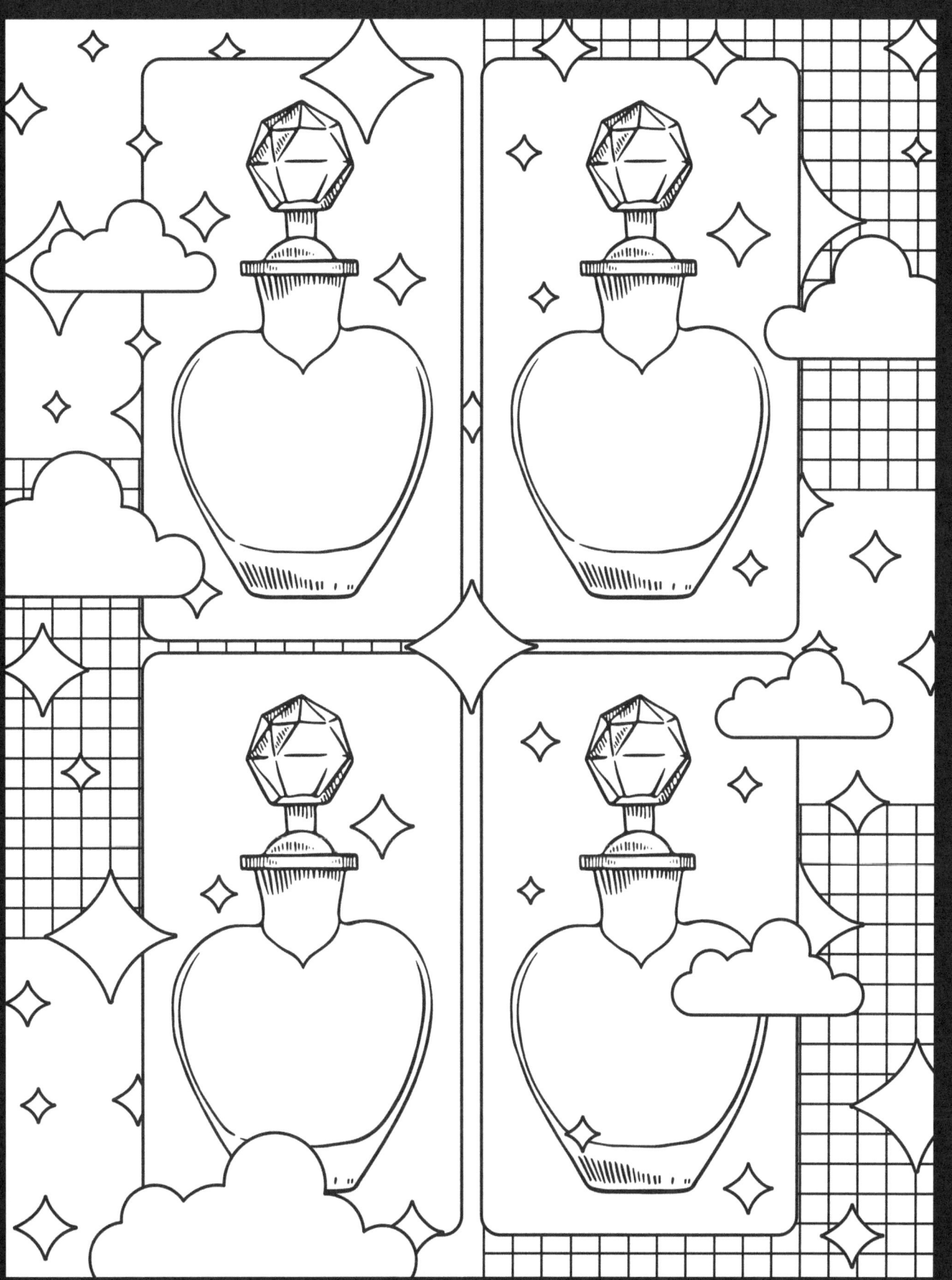

LABEL ME

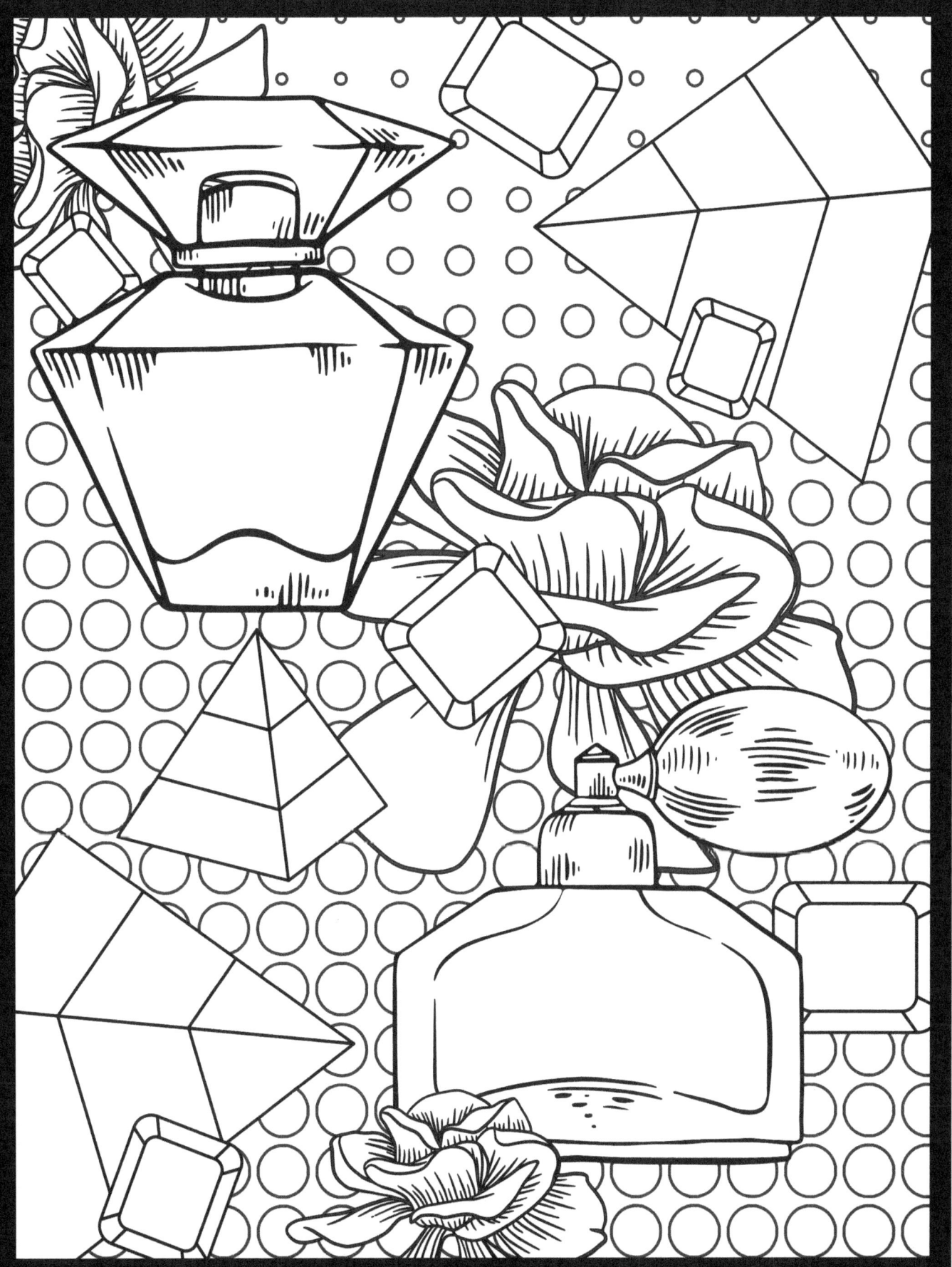

FABULOUS

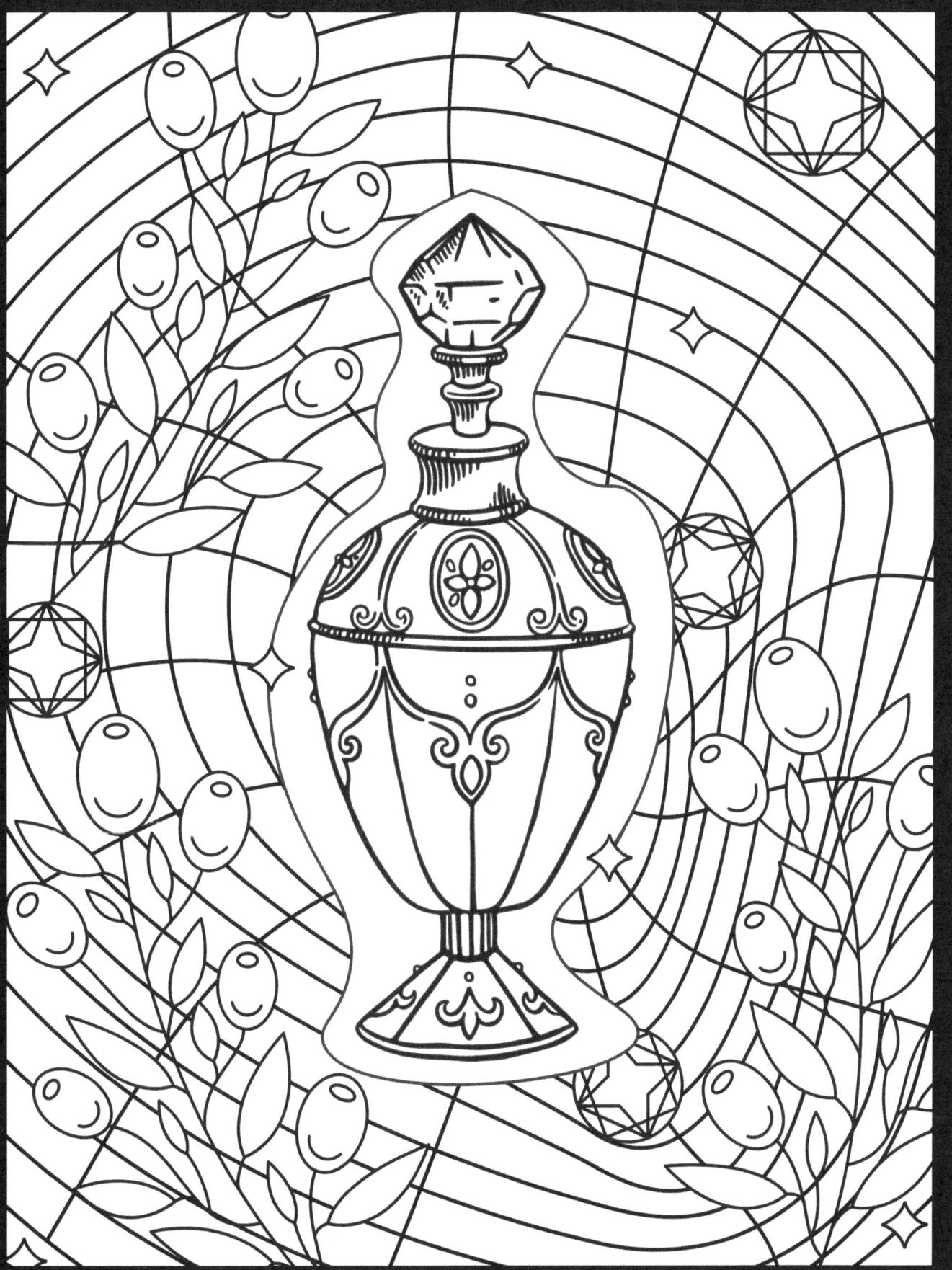

FRESH

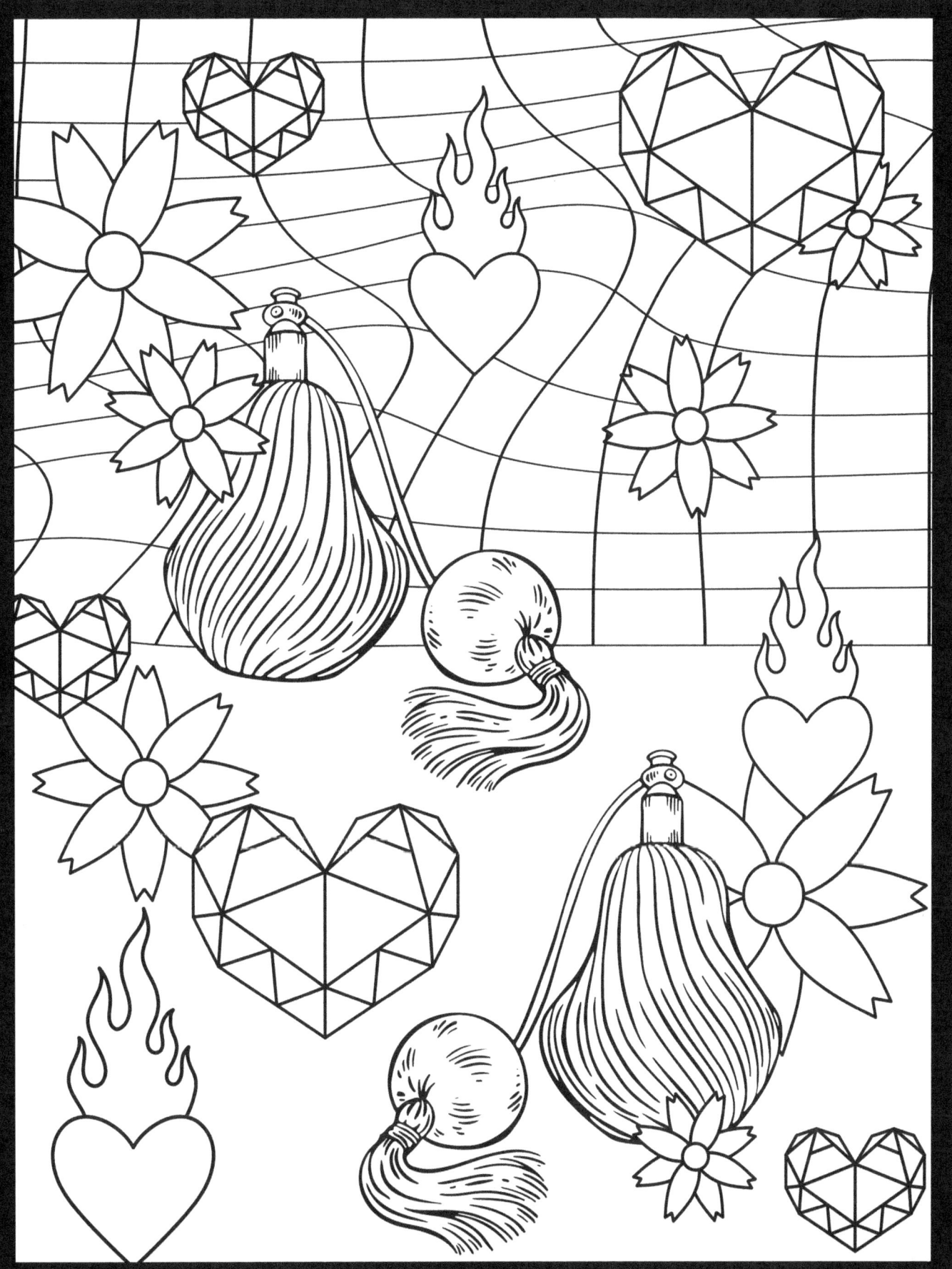

FIRE

NATURAL BEAUTY

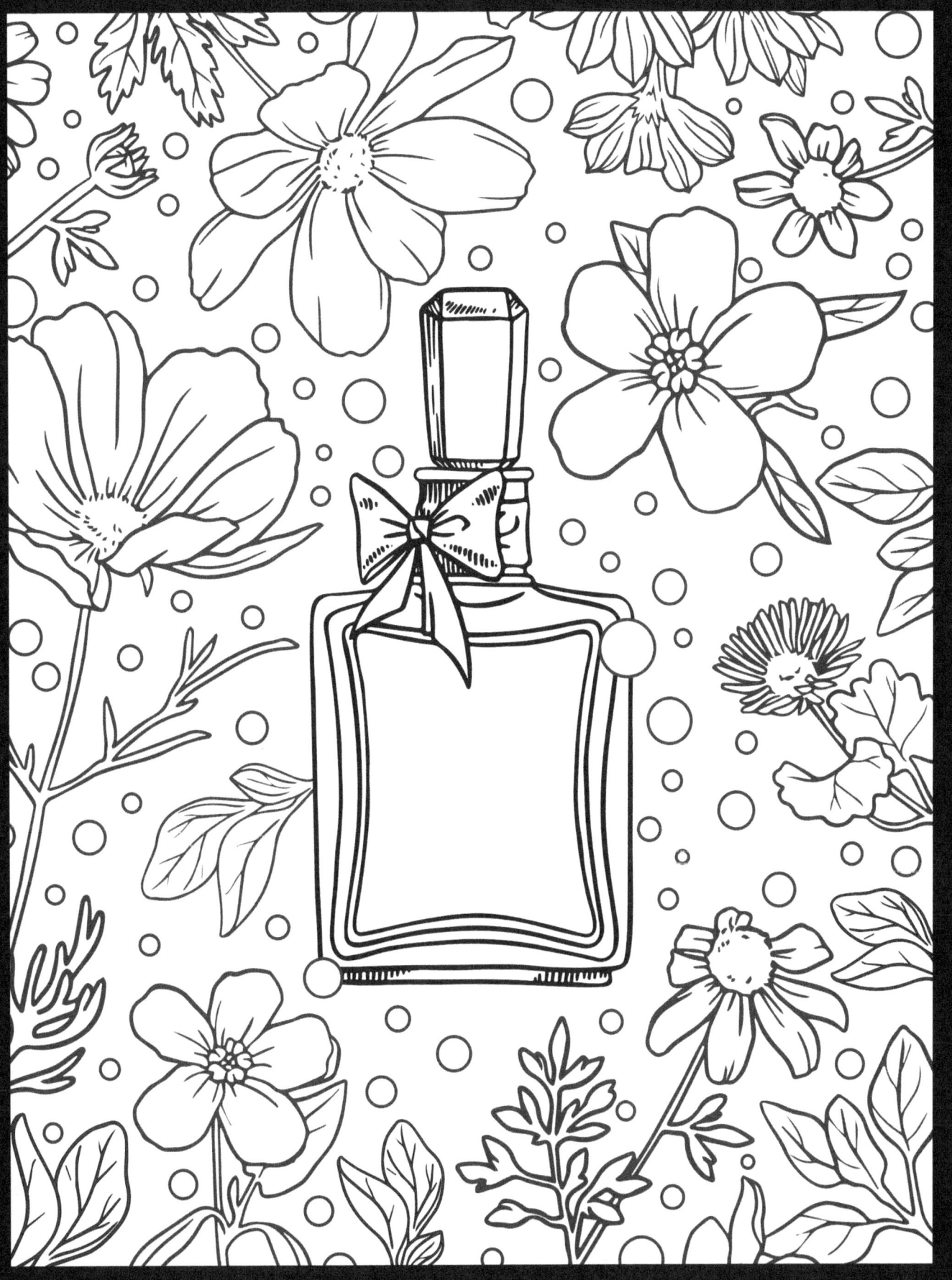

MAGNIFI SCENT LOL

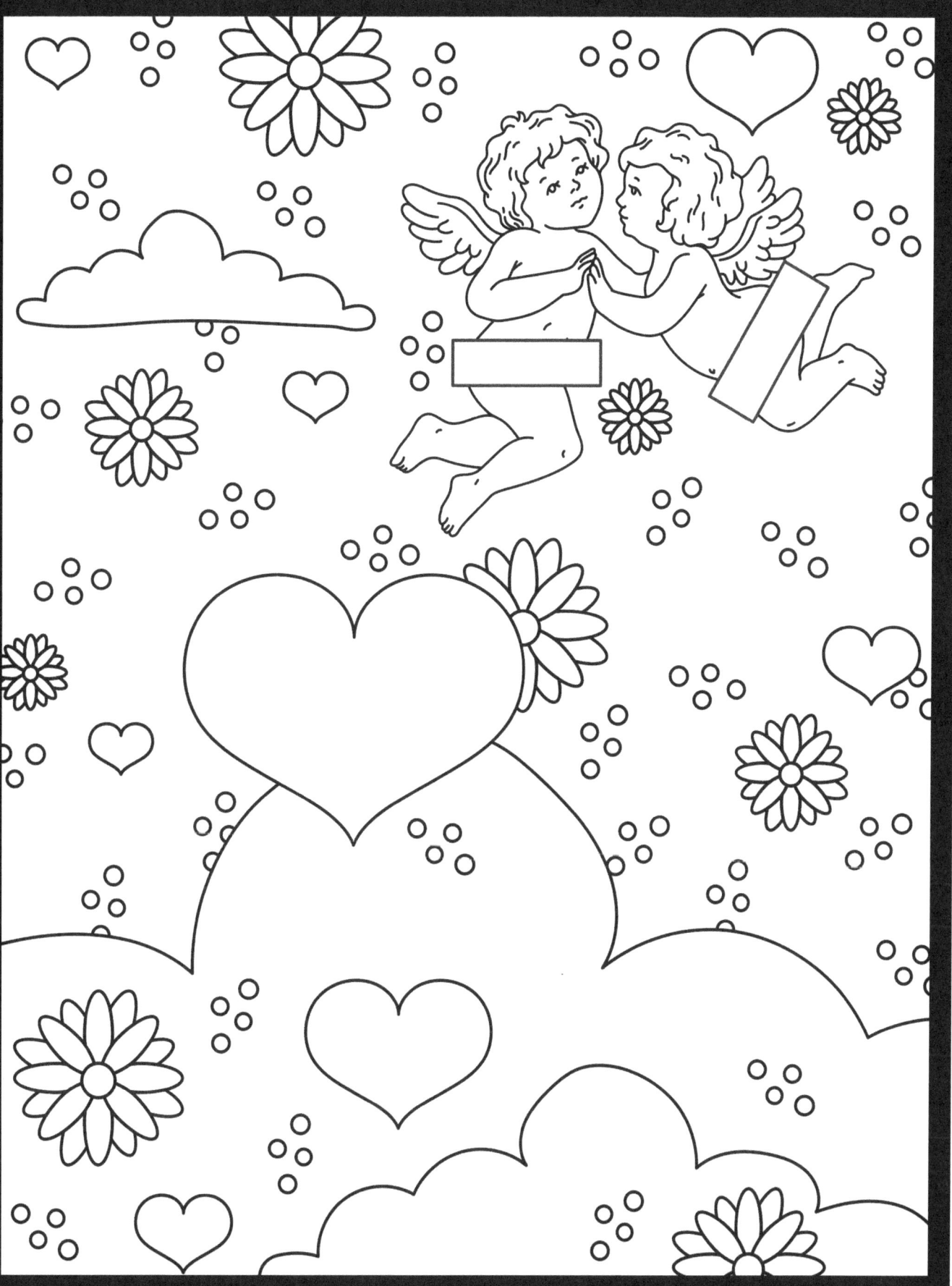

FULL OF HEART

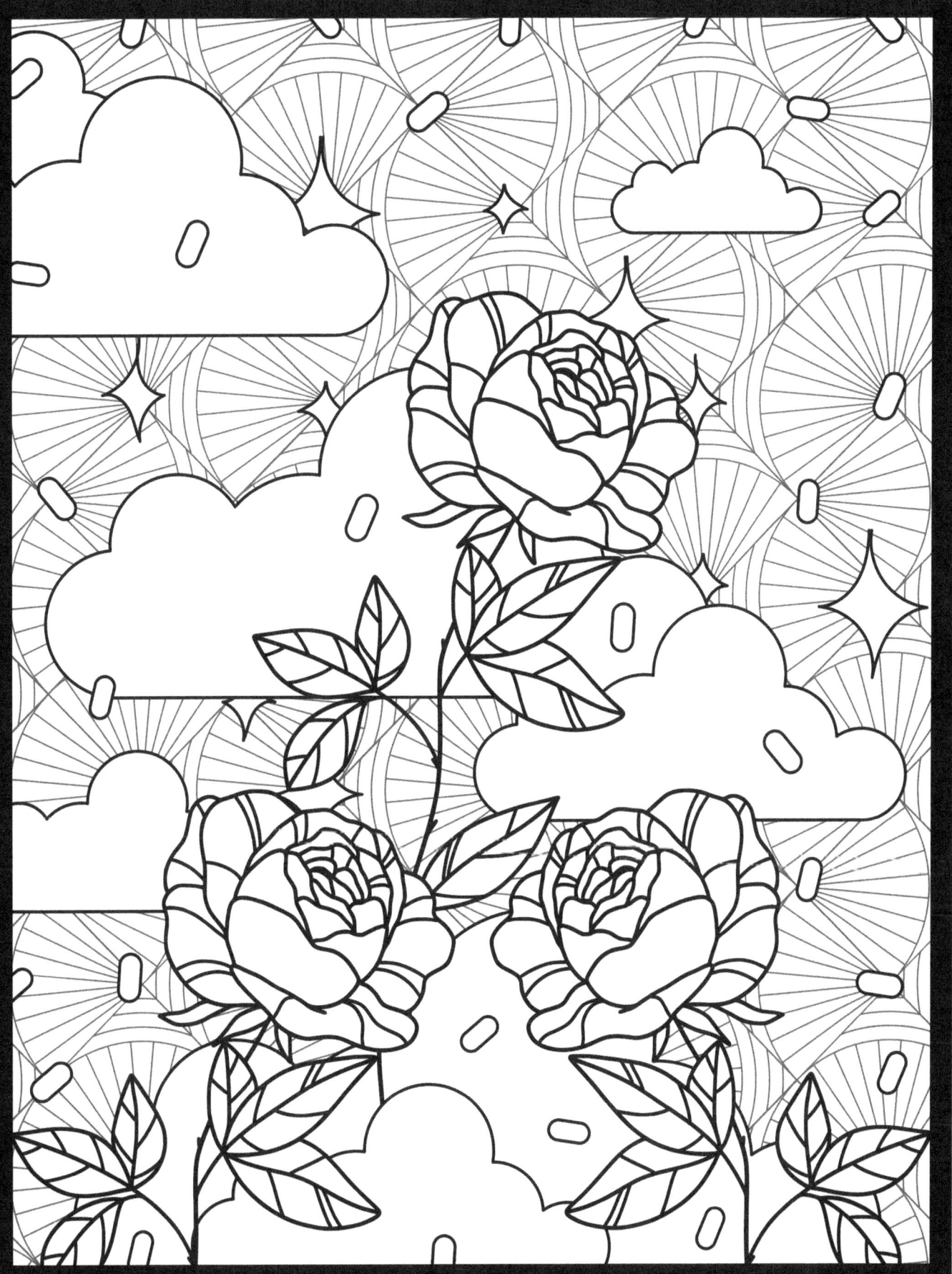

TRI ME

WE CAN GO IN ANY DIRECTION

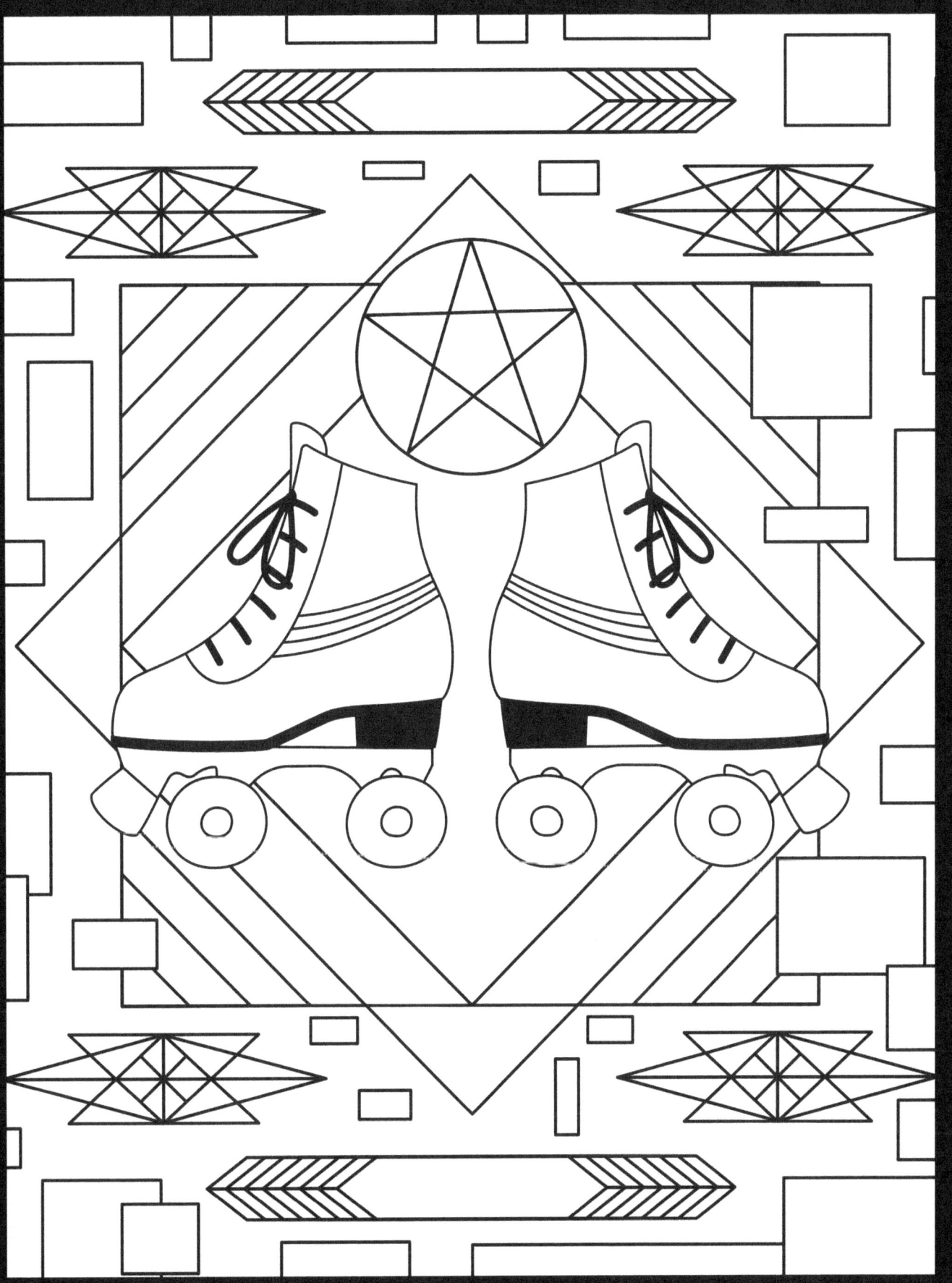

HOW I ROLL

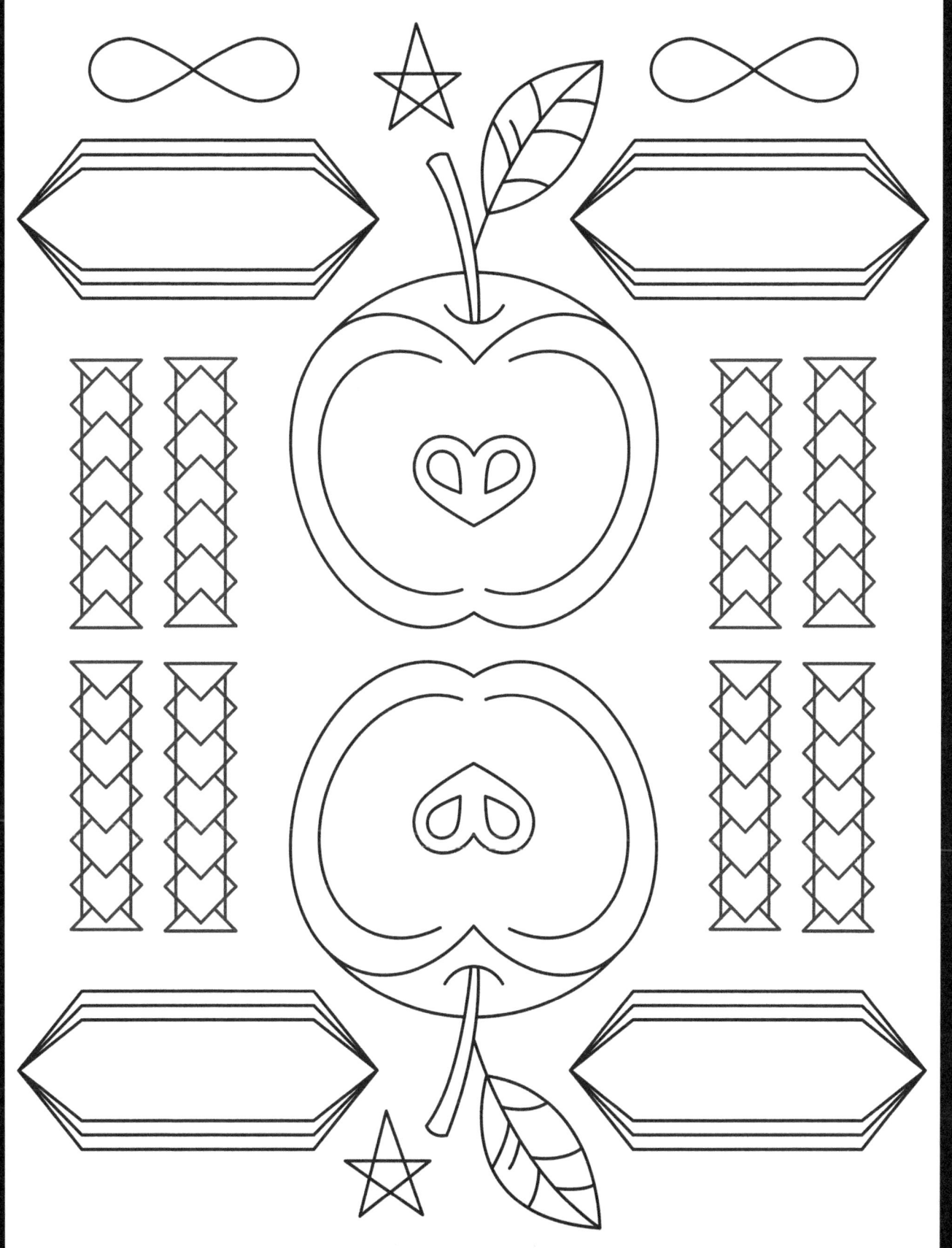

TAKE A BITE

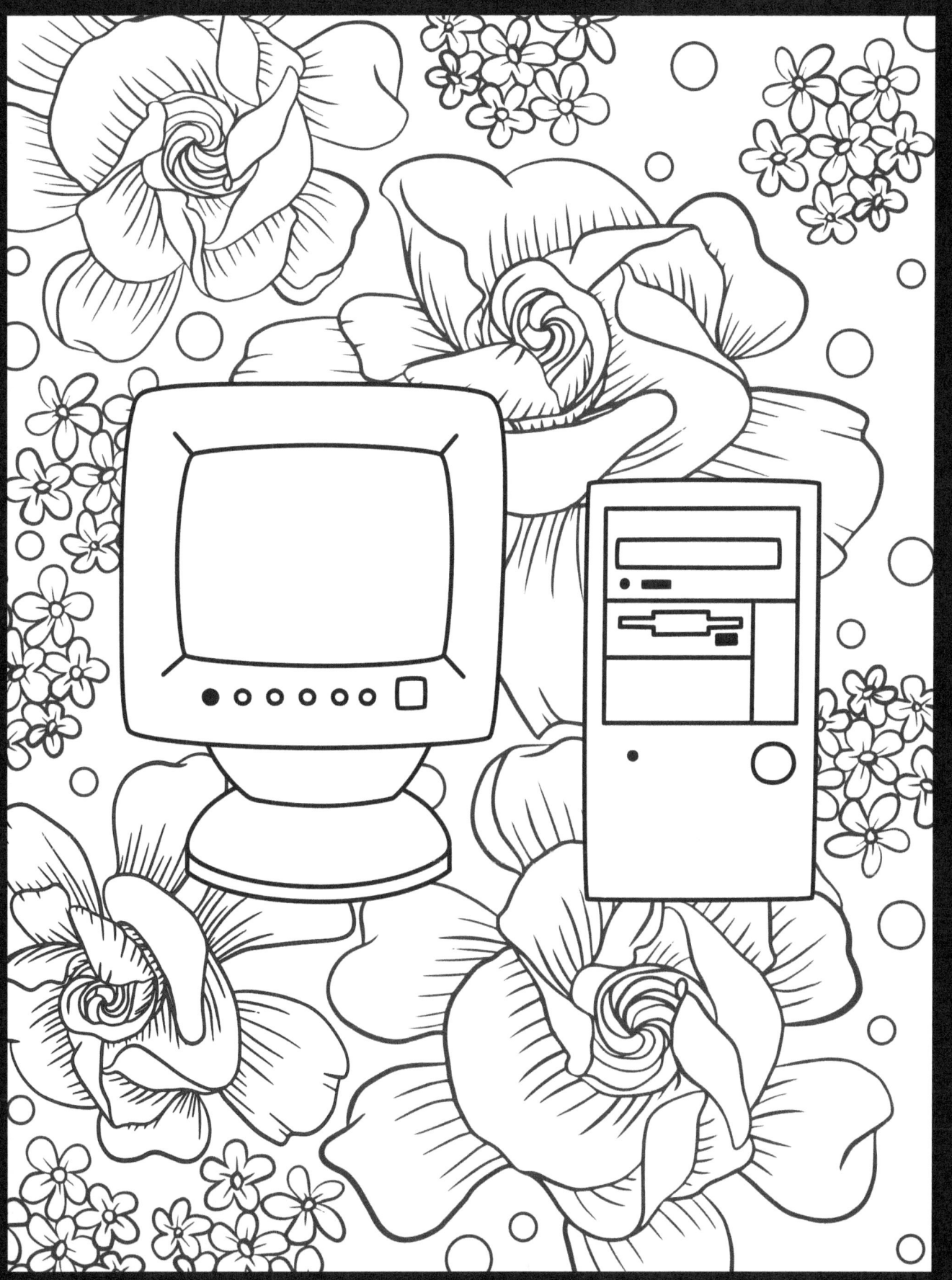

CANNOT COMPUTE

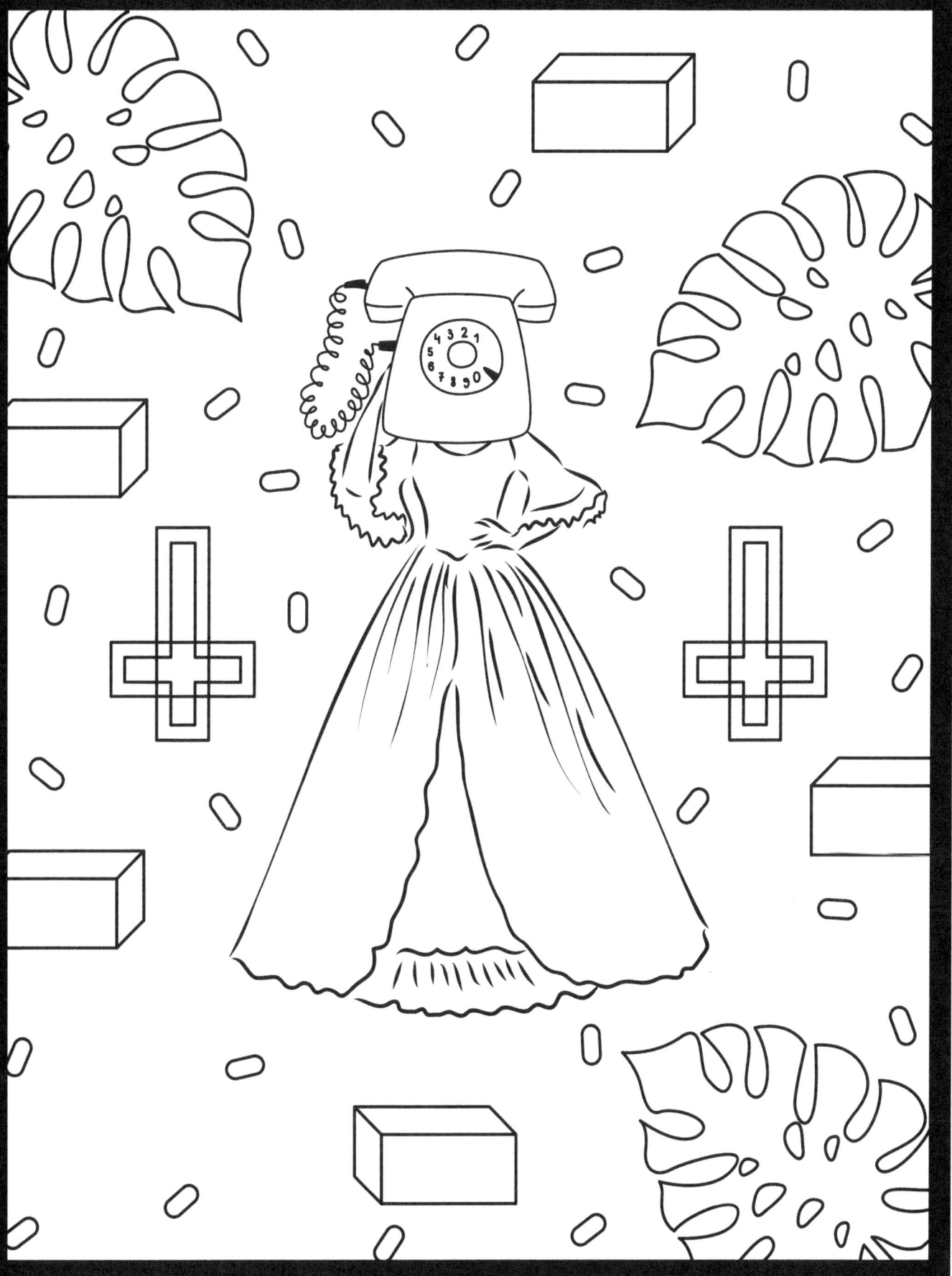

HANG UP

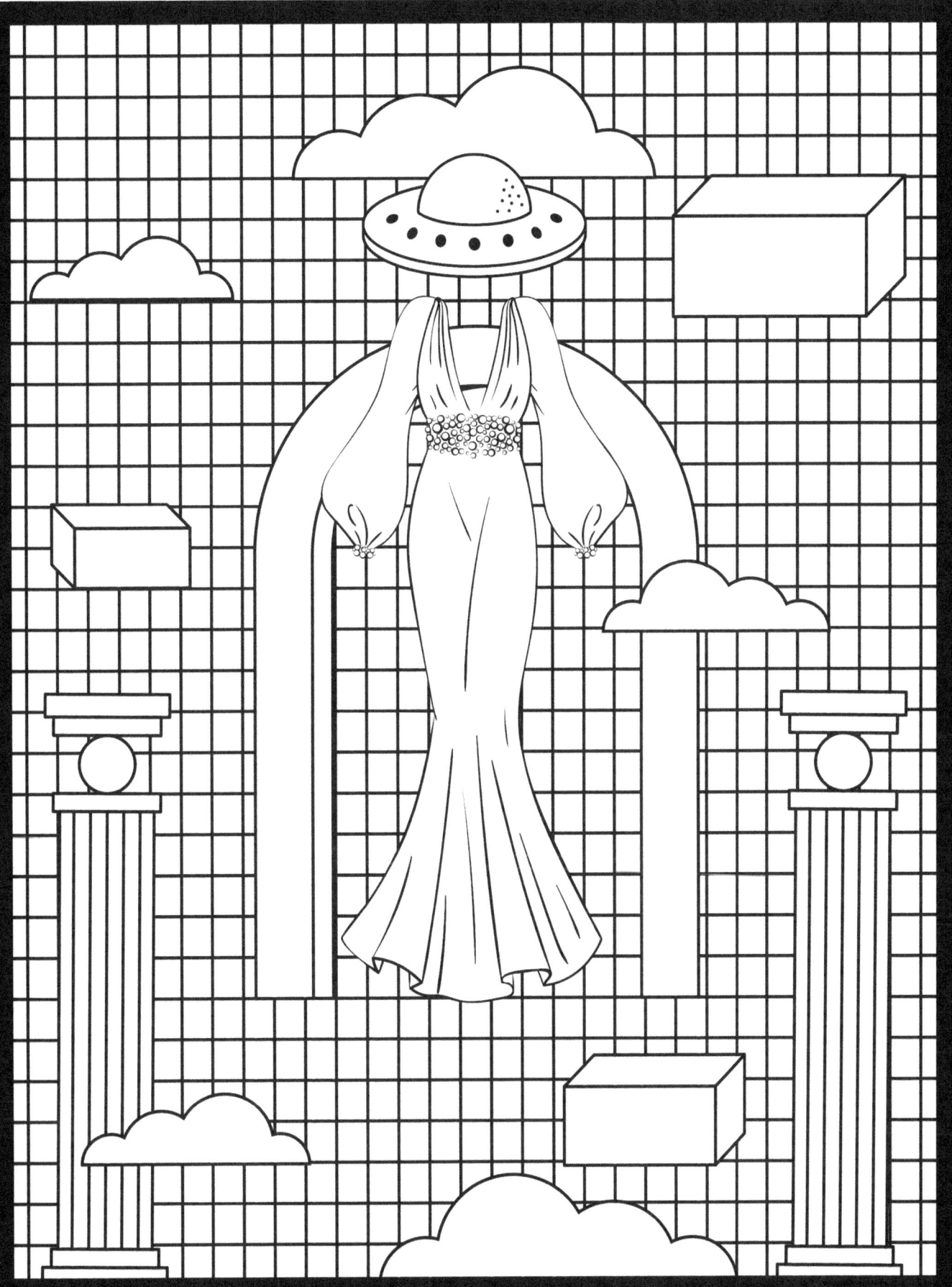

OUT OF THIS WORLD

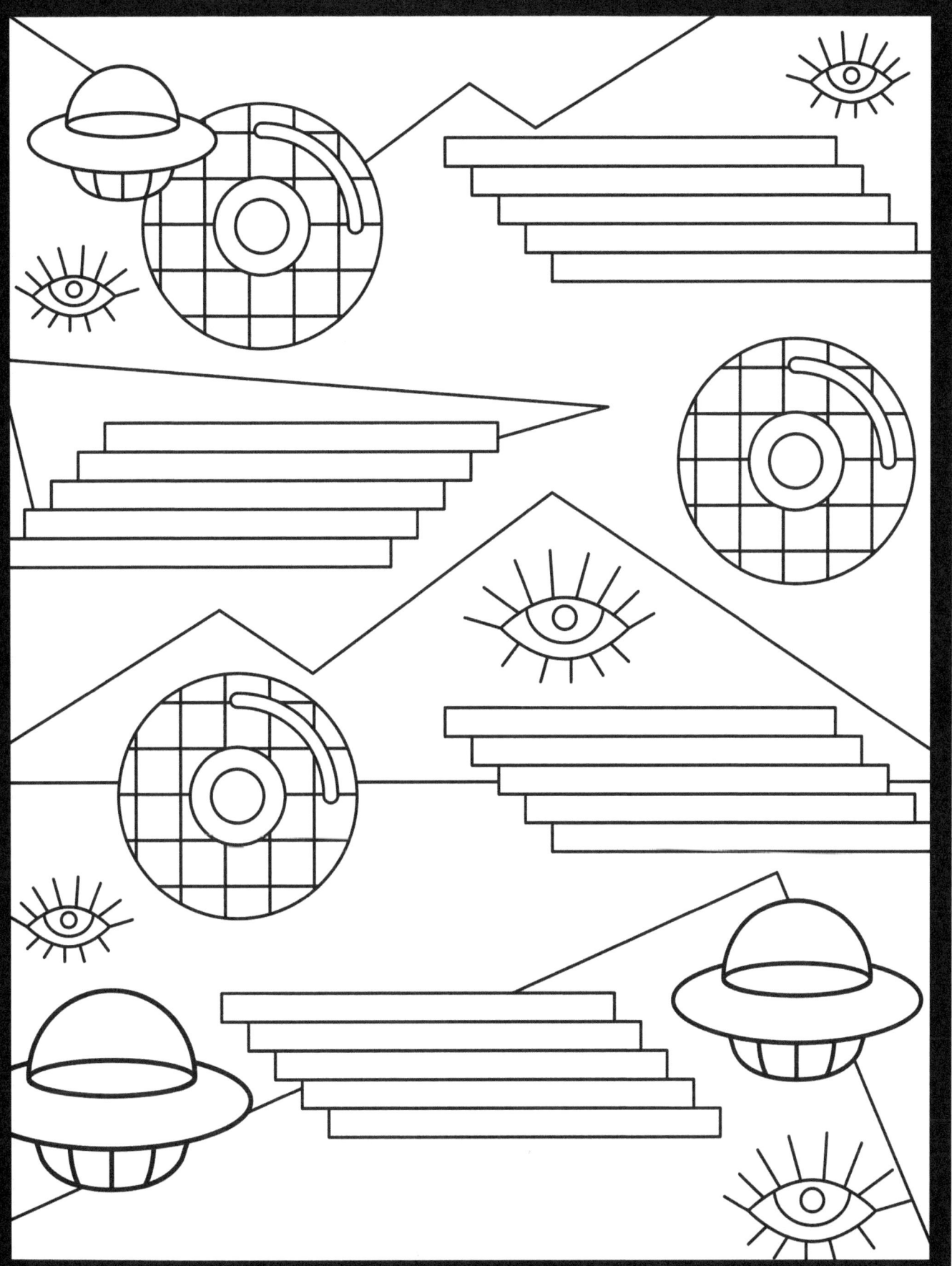

DISCOVERY

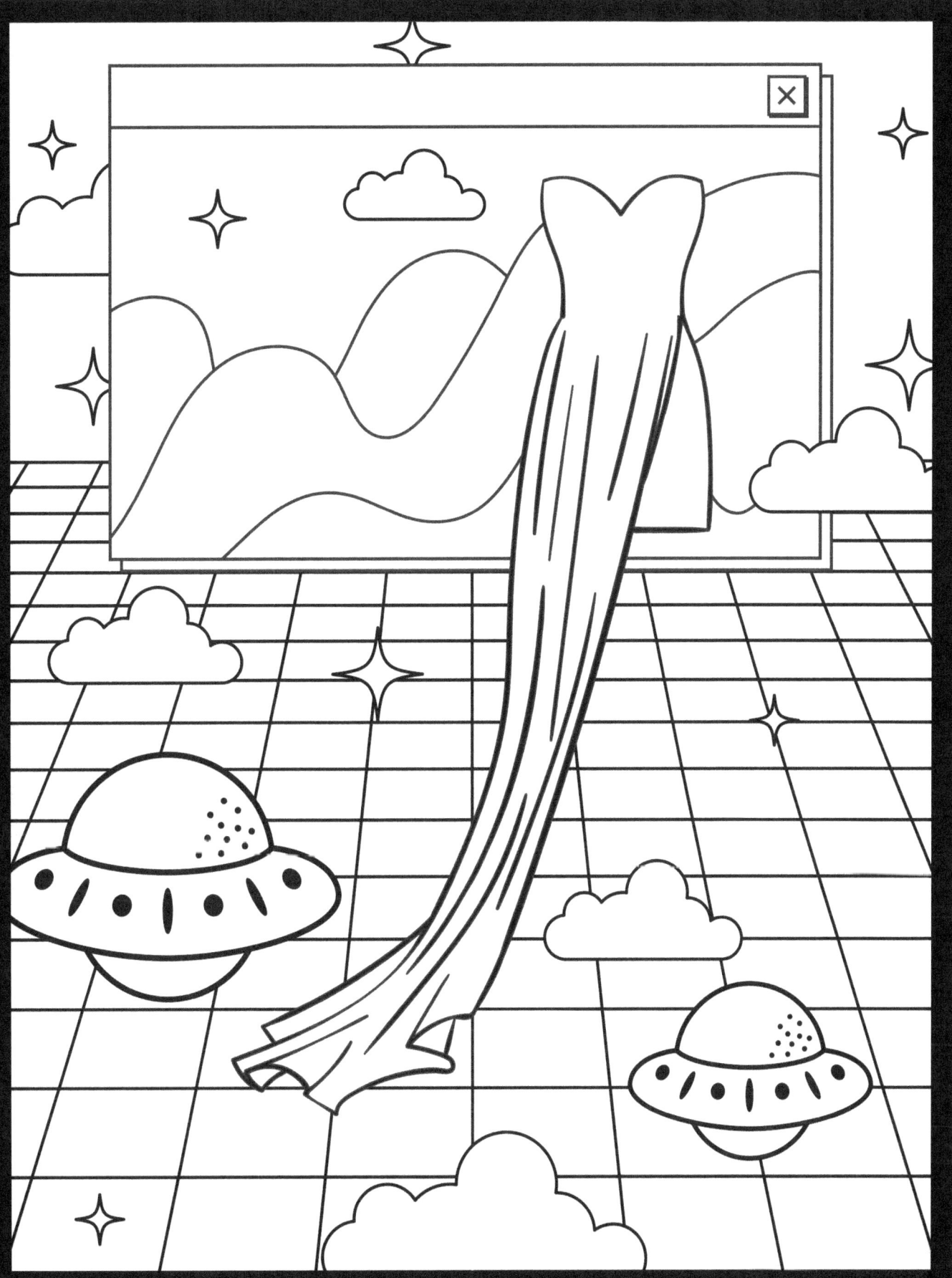

HOW LONG

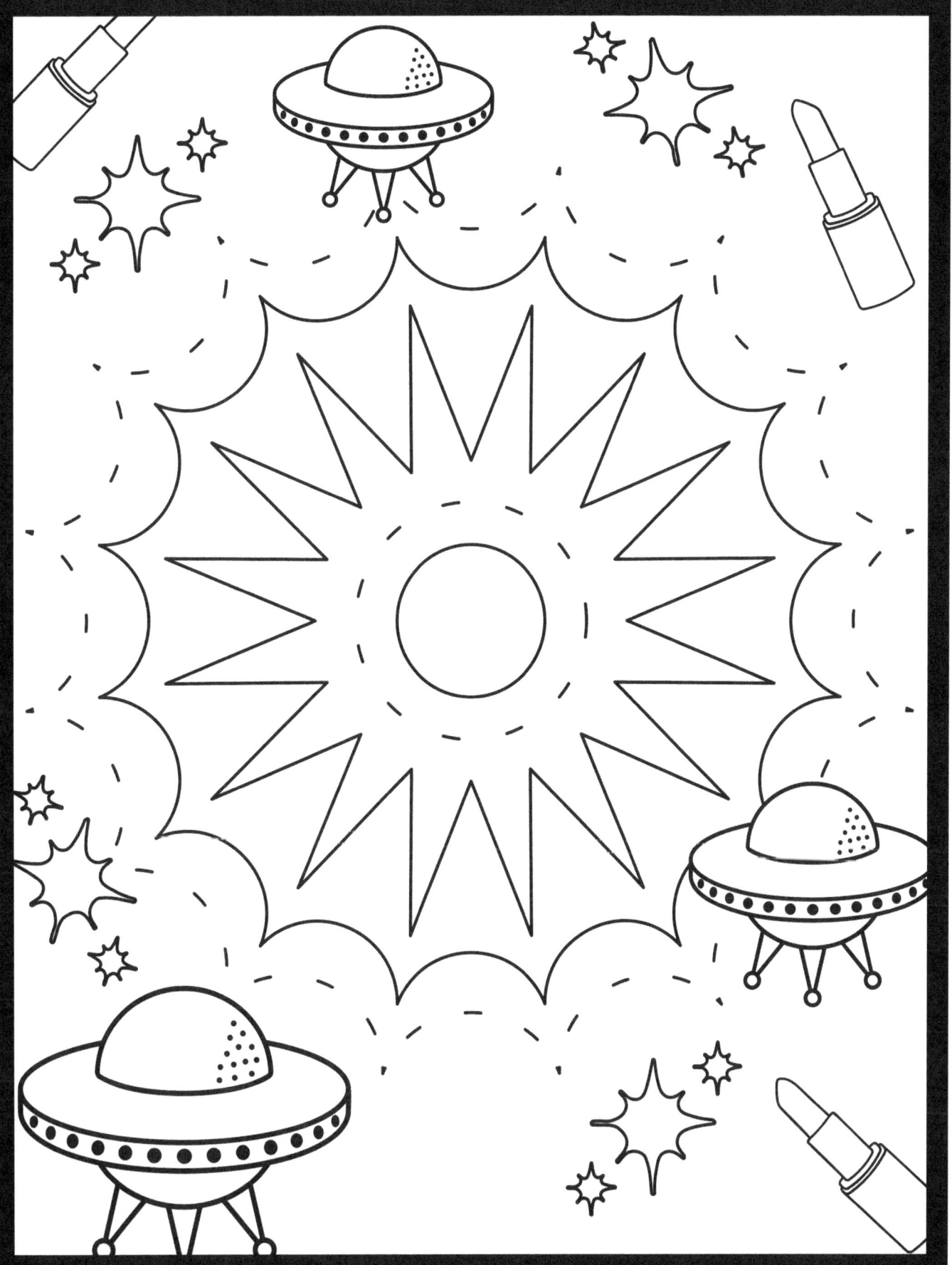

ARE WE THERE YET

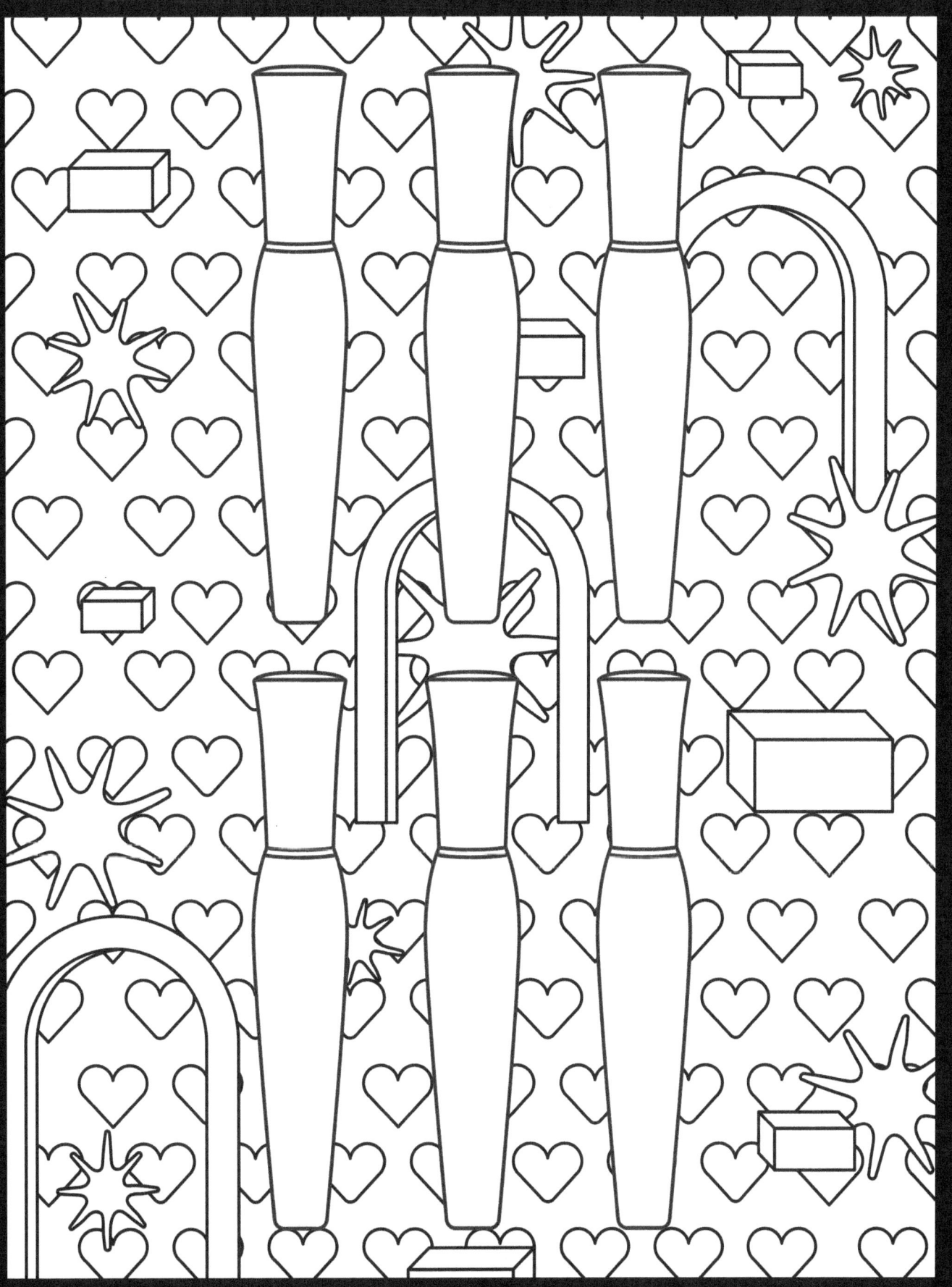

BLACKOUT

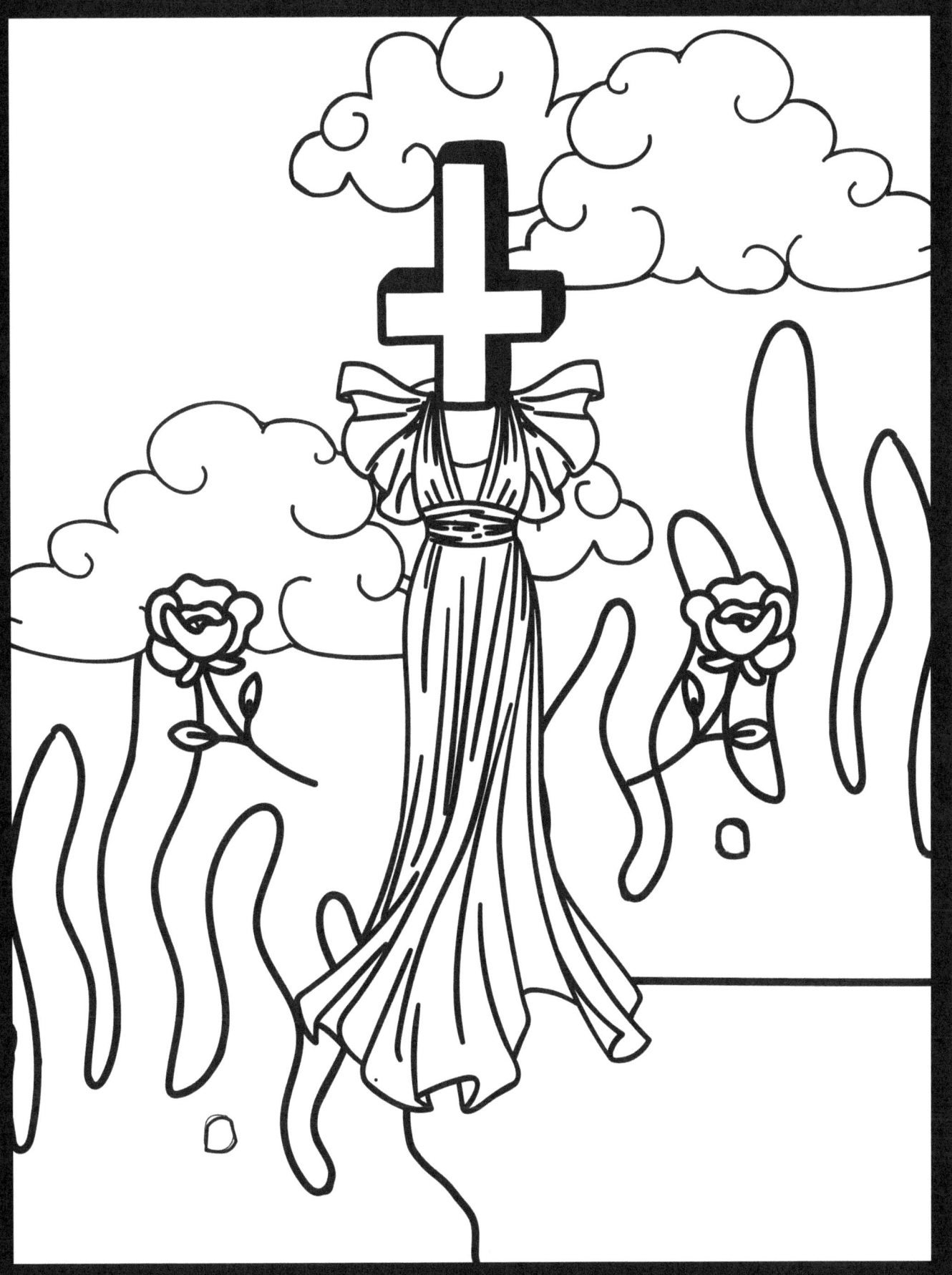

CRUCIFIED

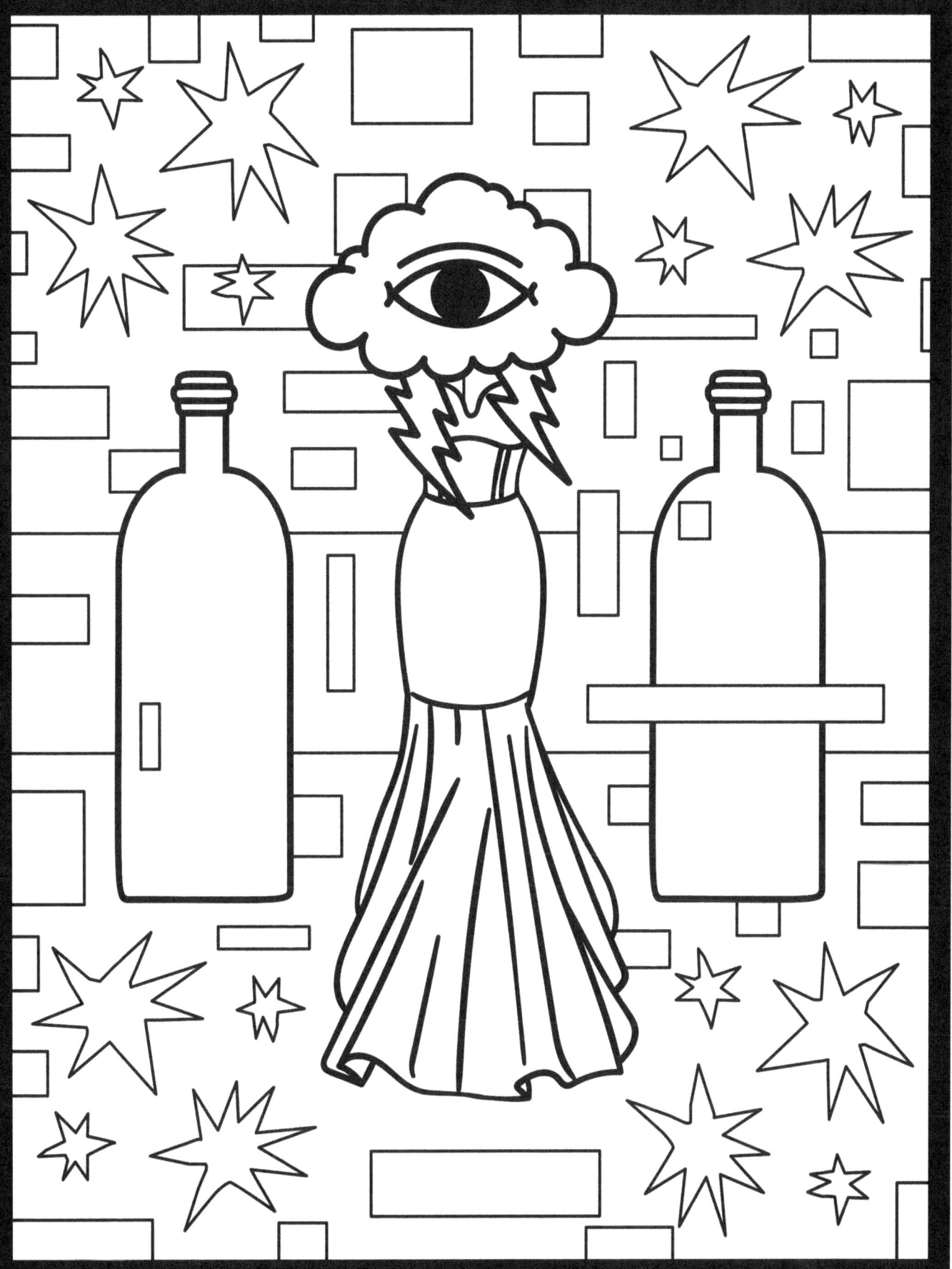

LIGHTNING IN A BOTTLE

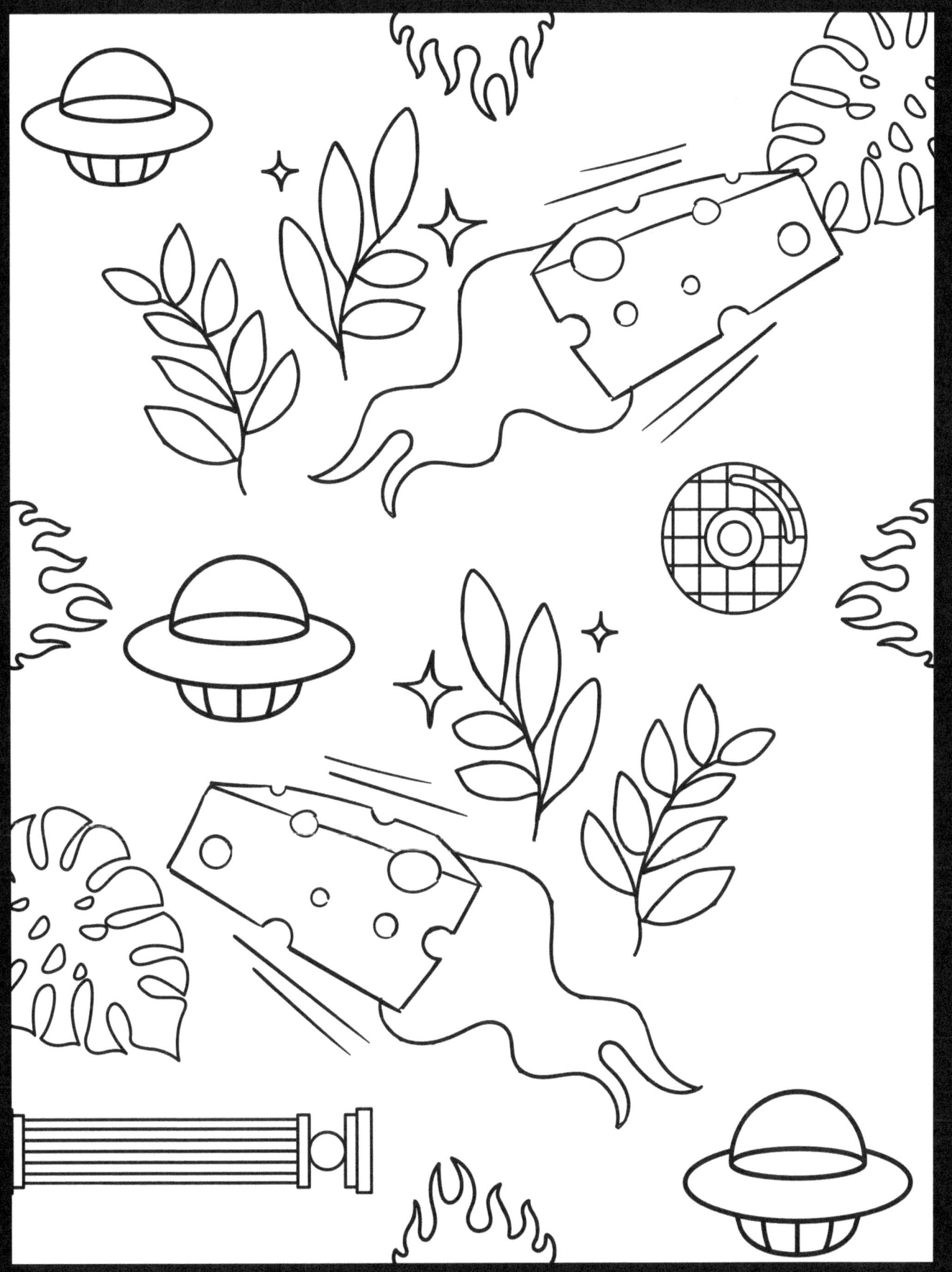

GET THE CHEESE

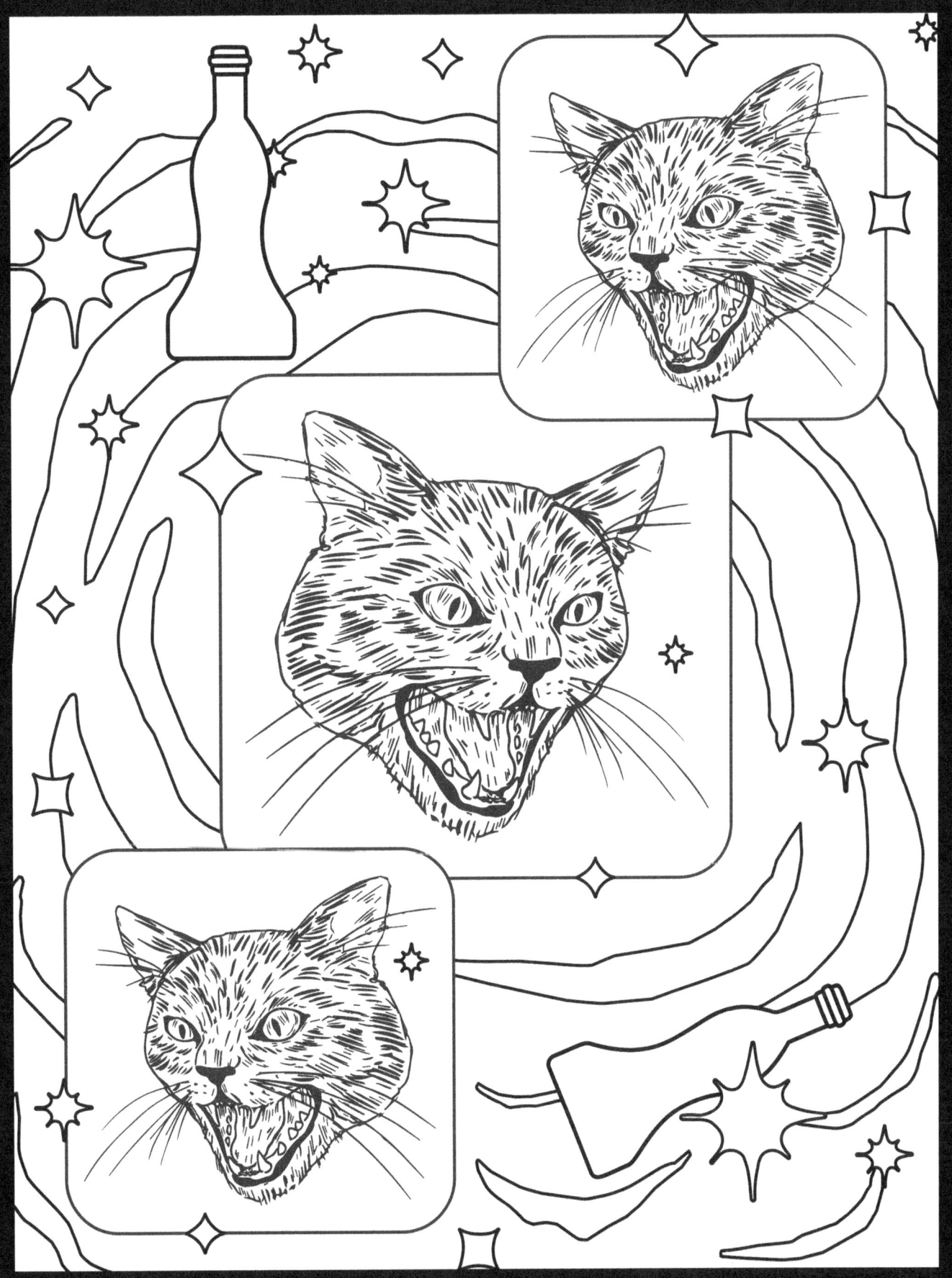

HISS

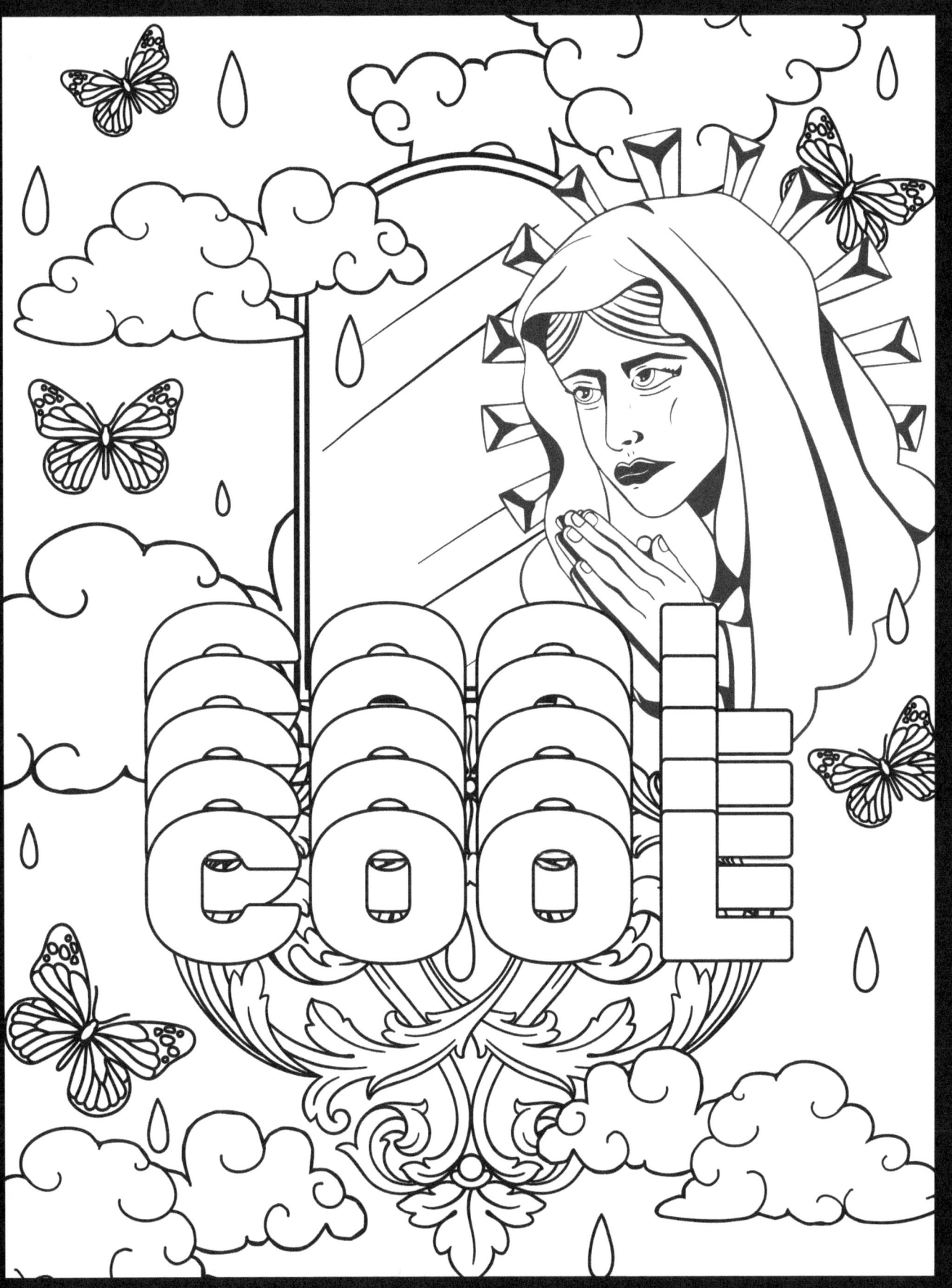

THIS IS COOL THIS IS FINE

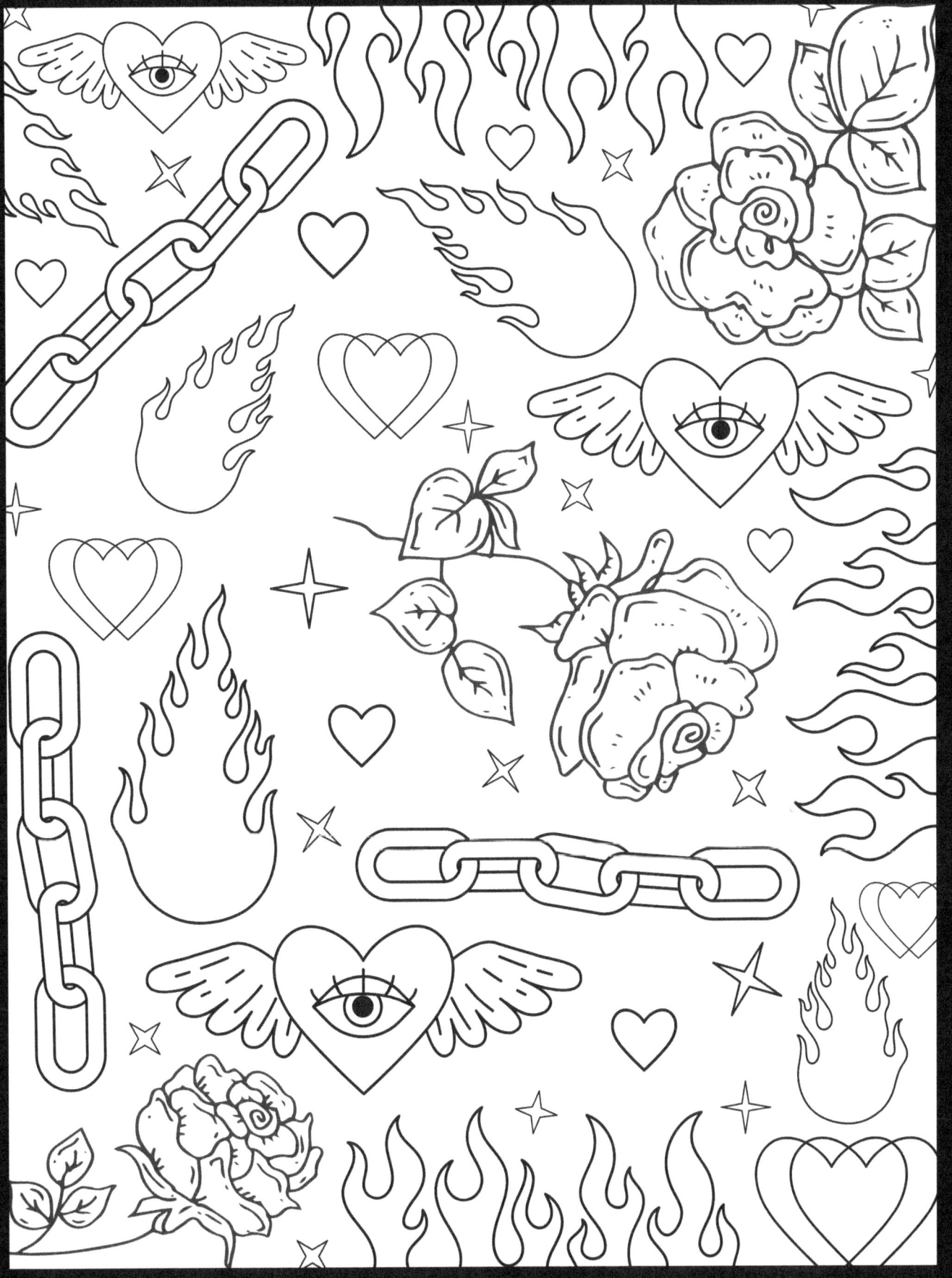

FLAMING HOT

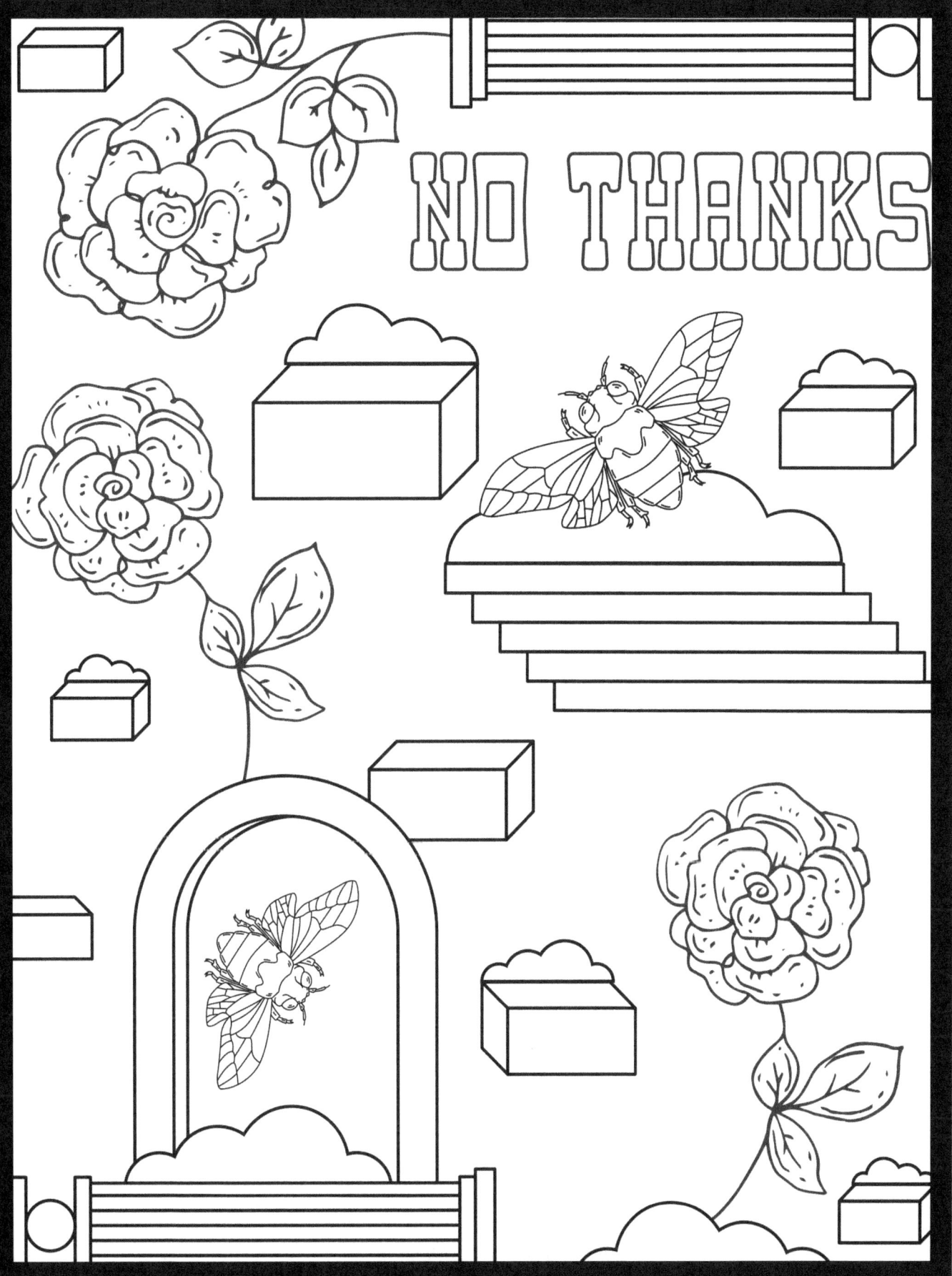

I WILL PASS

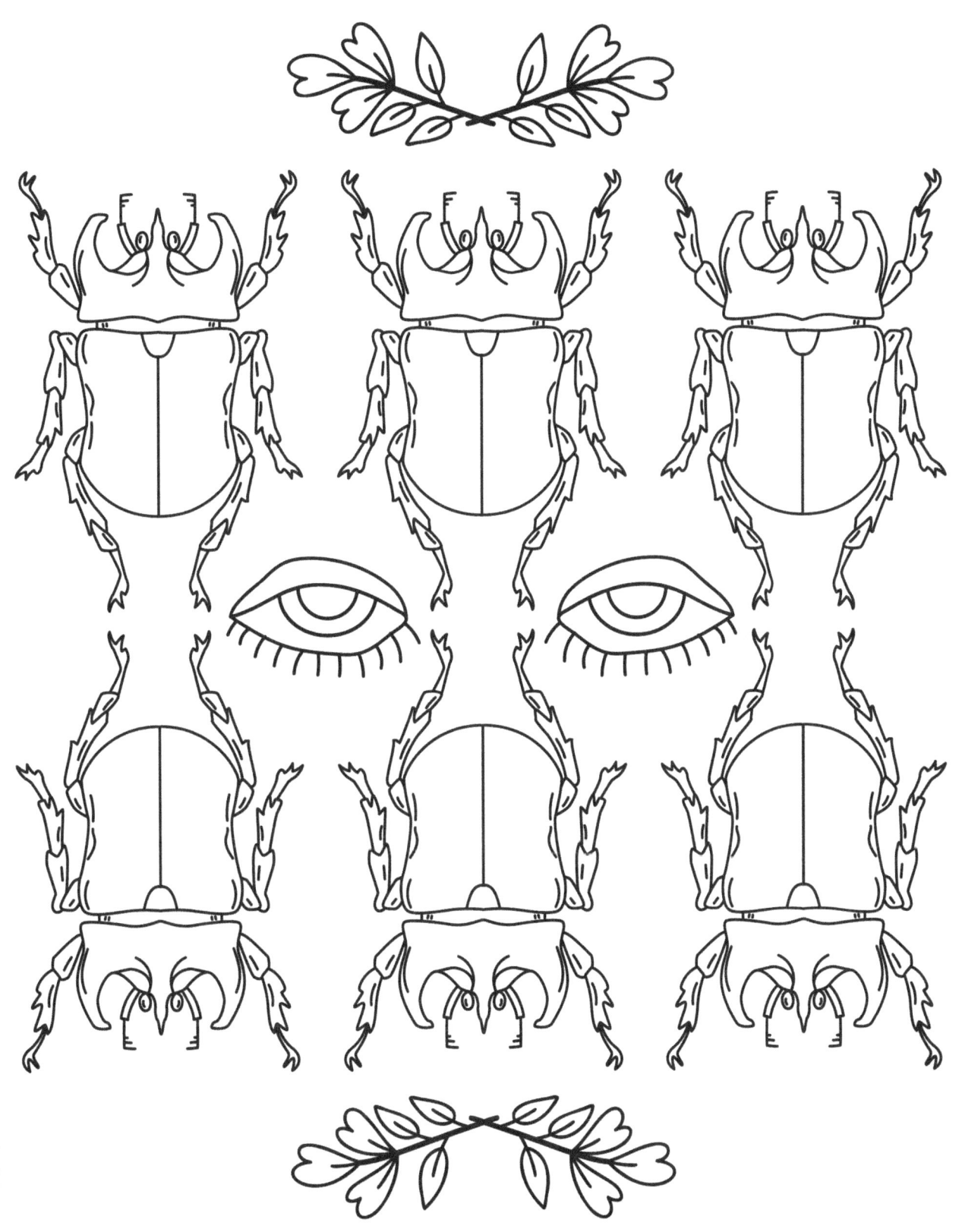

BEAUTY IS IN THE EYE

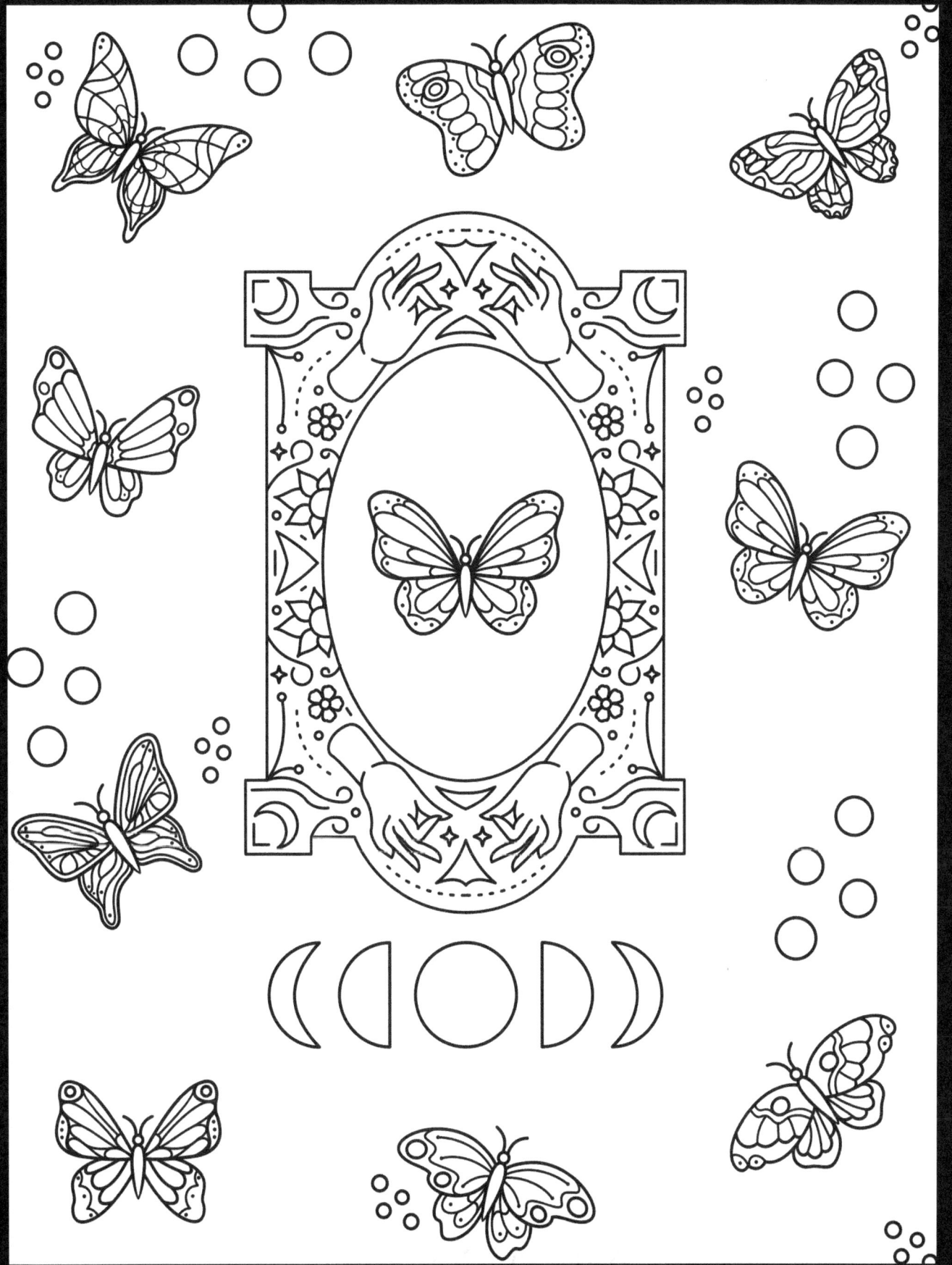

NATURAL DOORWAYS

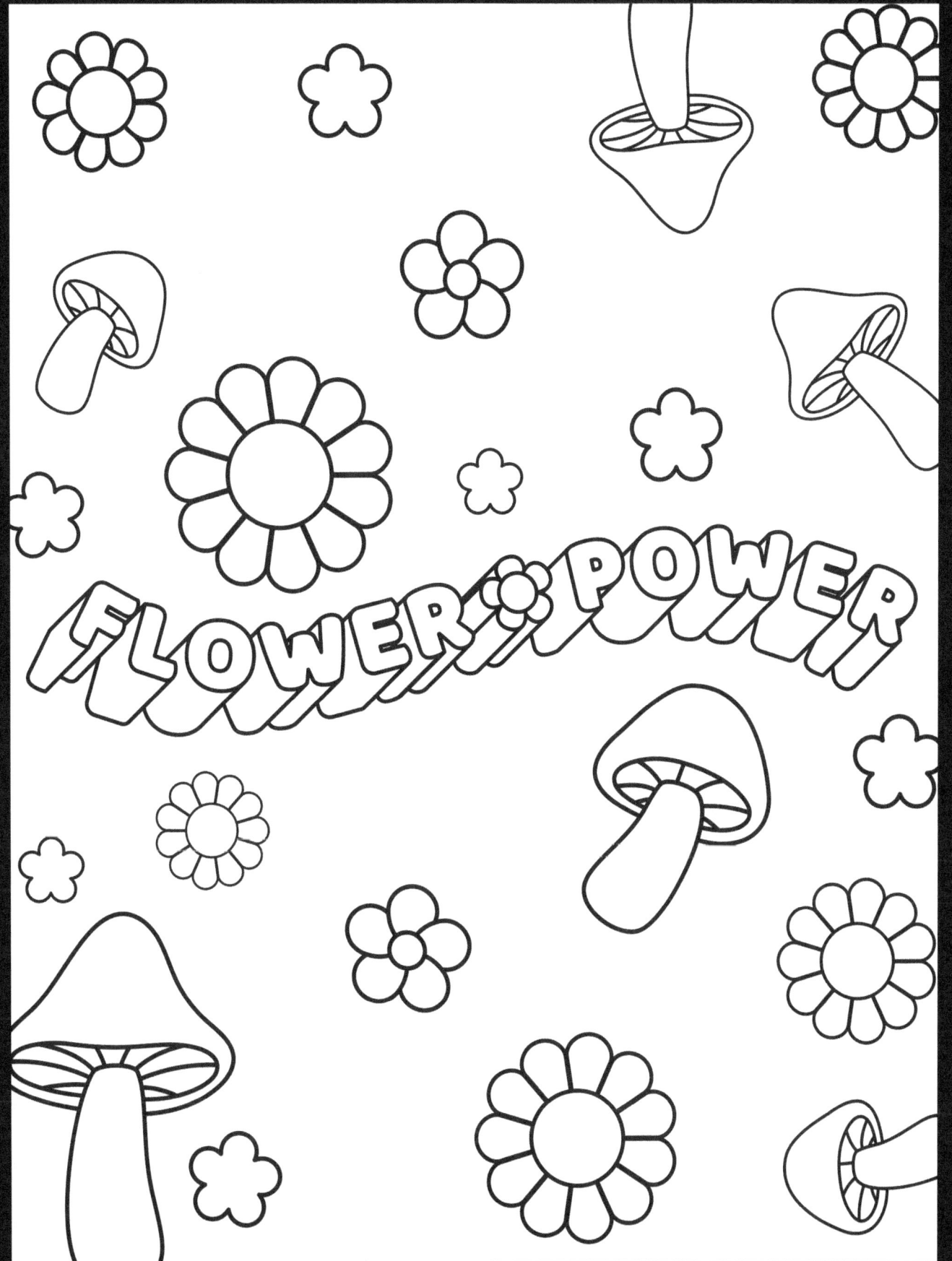

FLOWER POWER

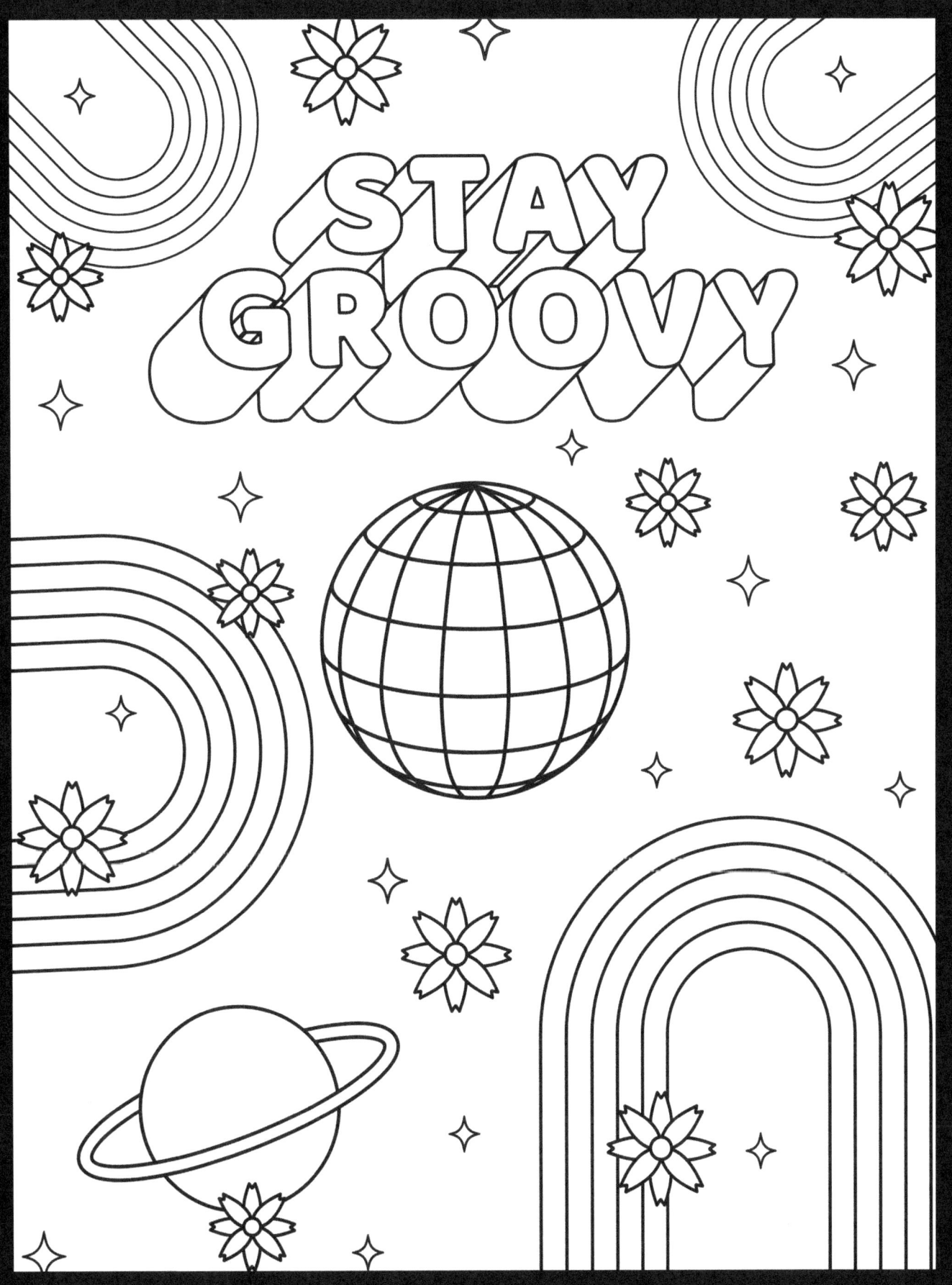

GROOVY BABY

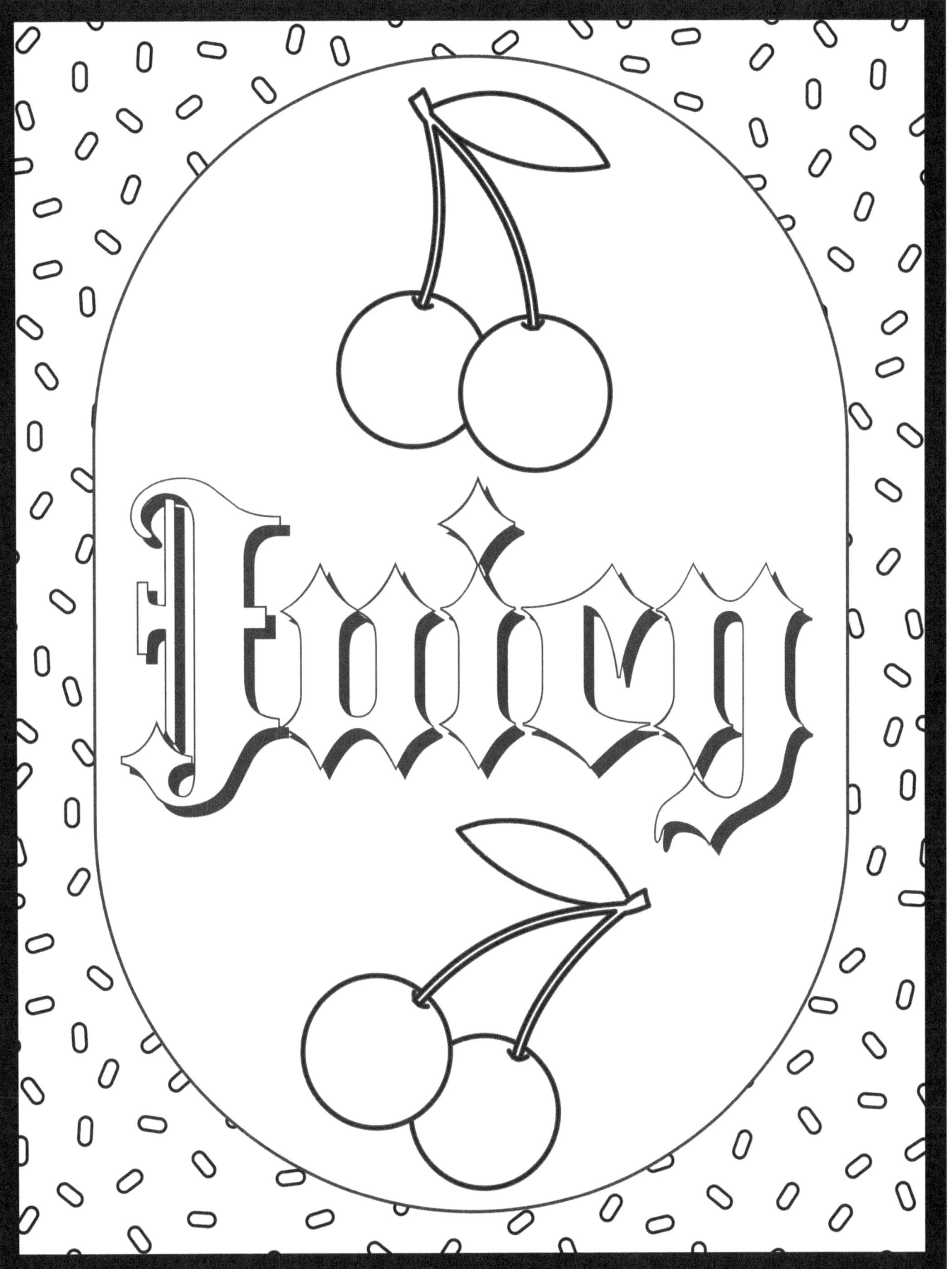

JUICY AF

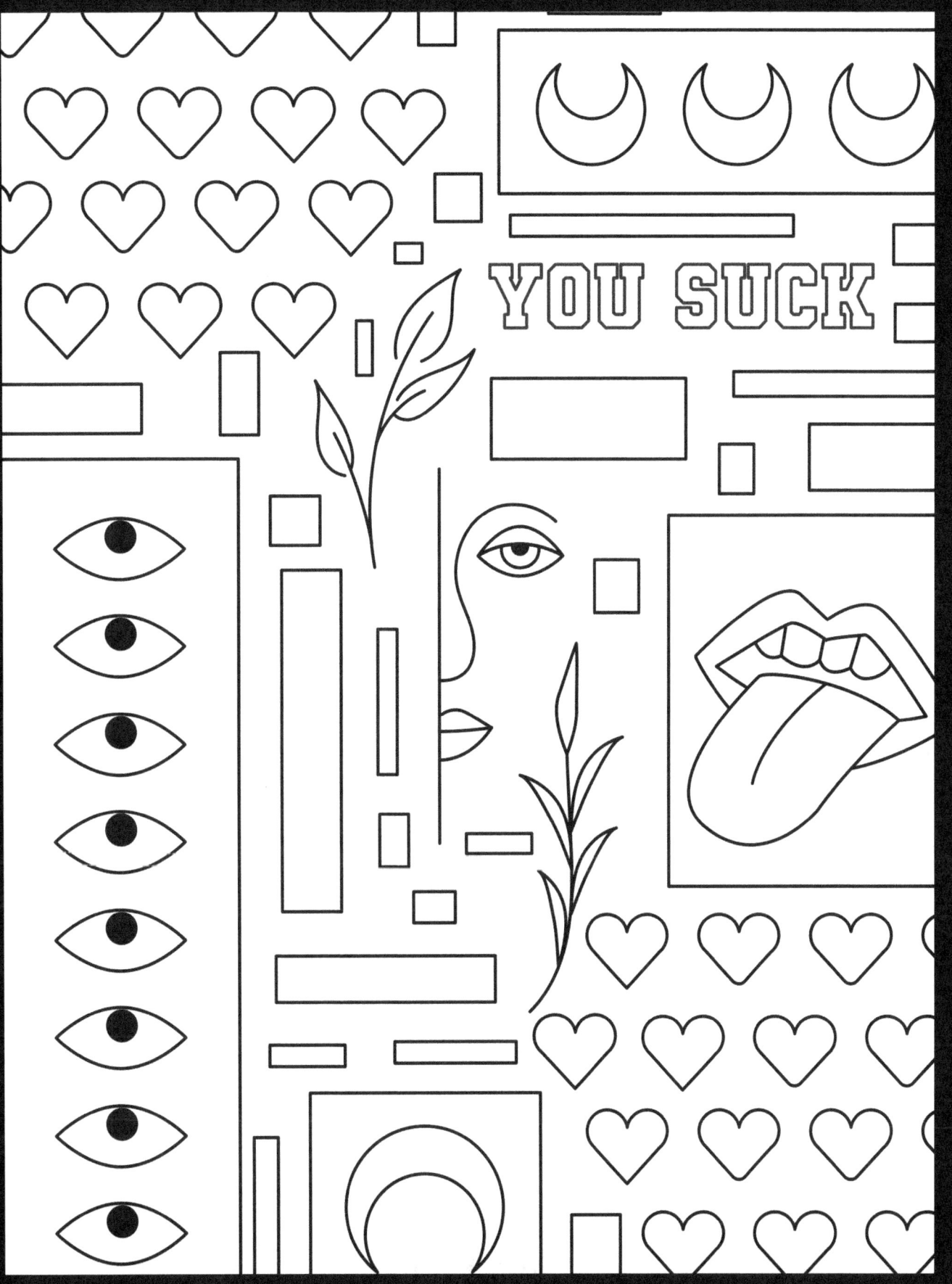

YOU SUCK

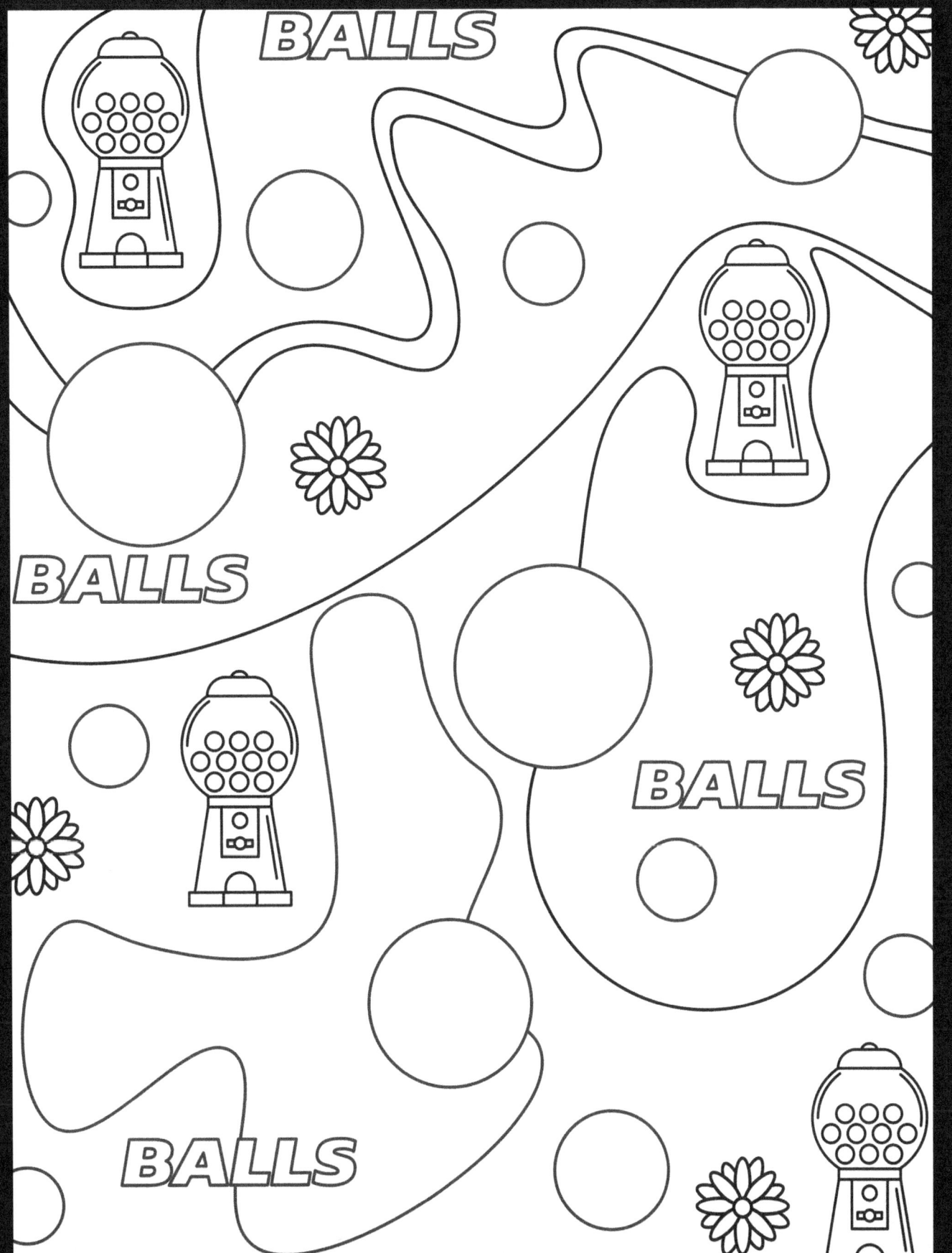

BALLS

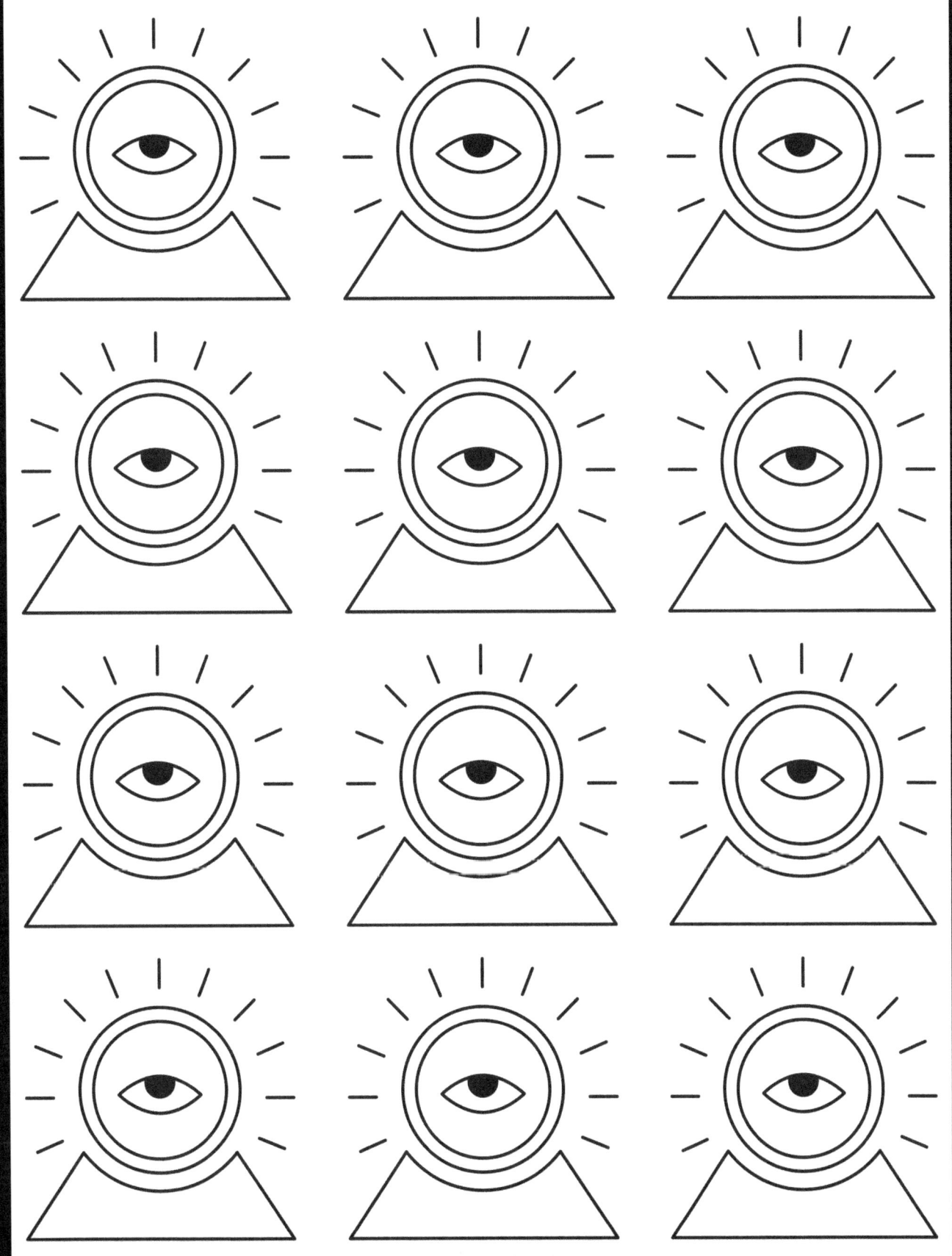

I PREDICTED THIS

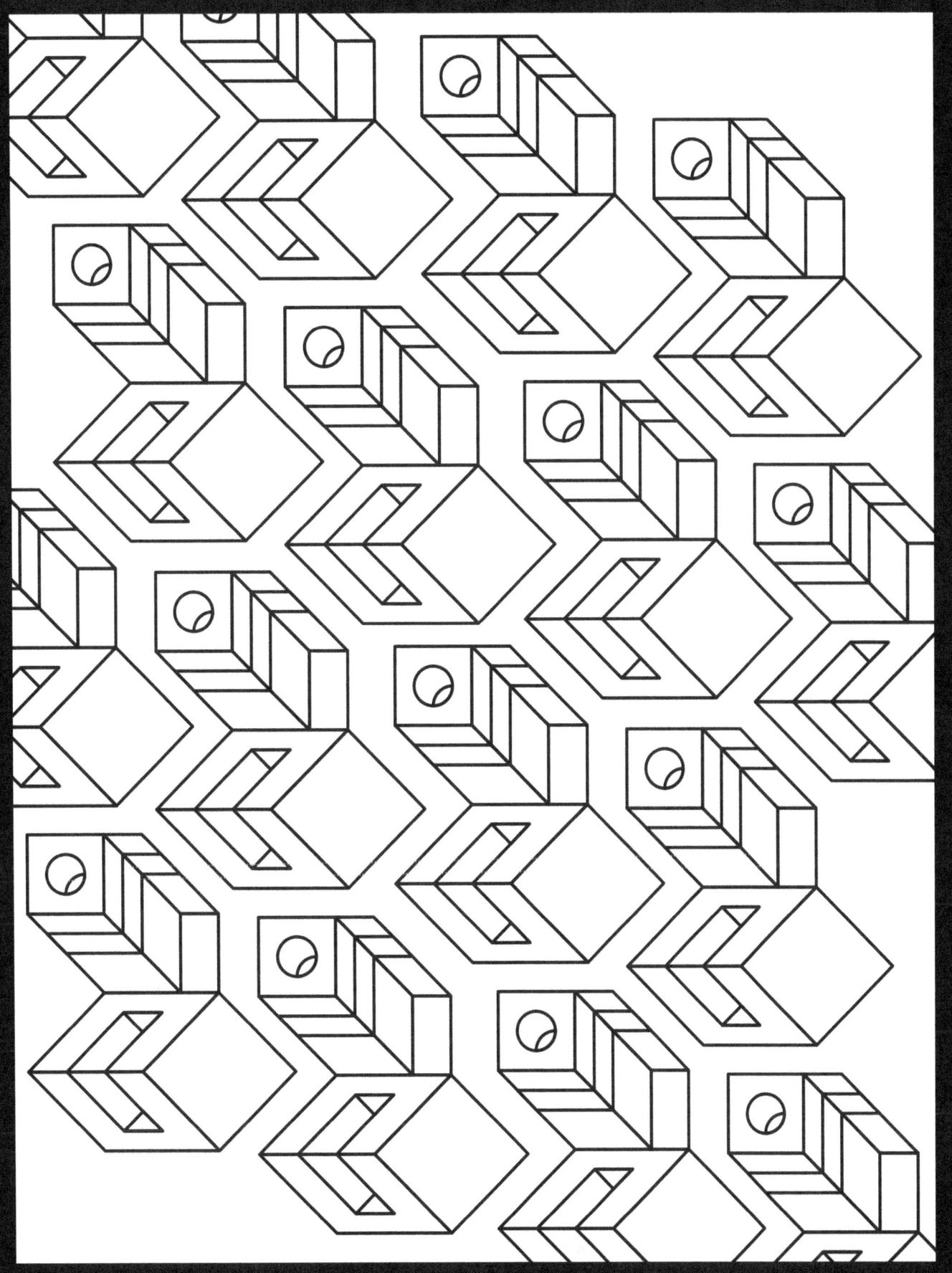

PATTERNS REPEAT

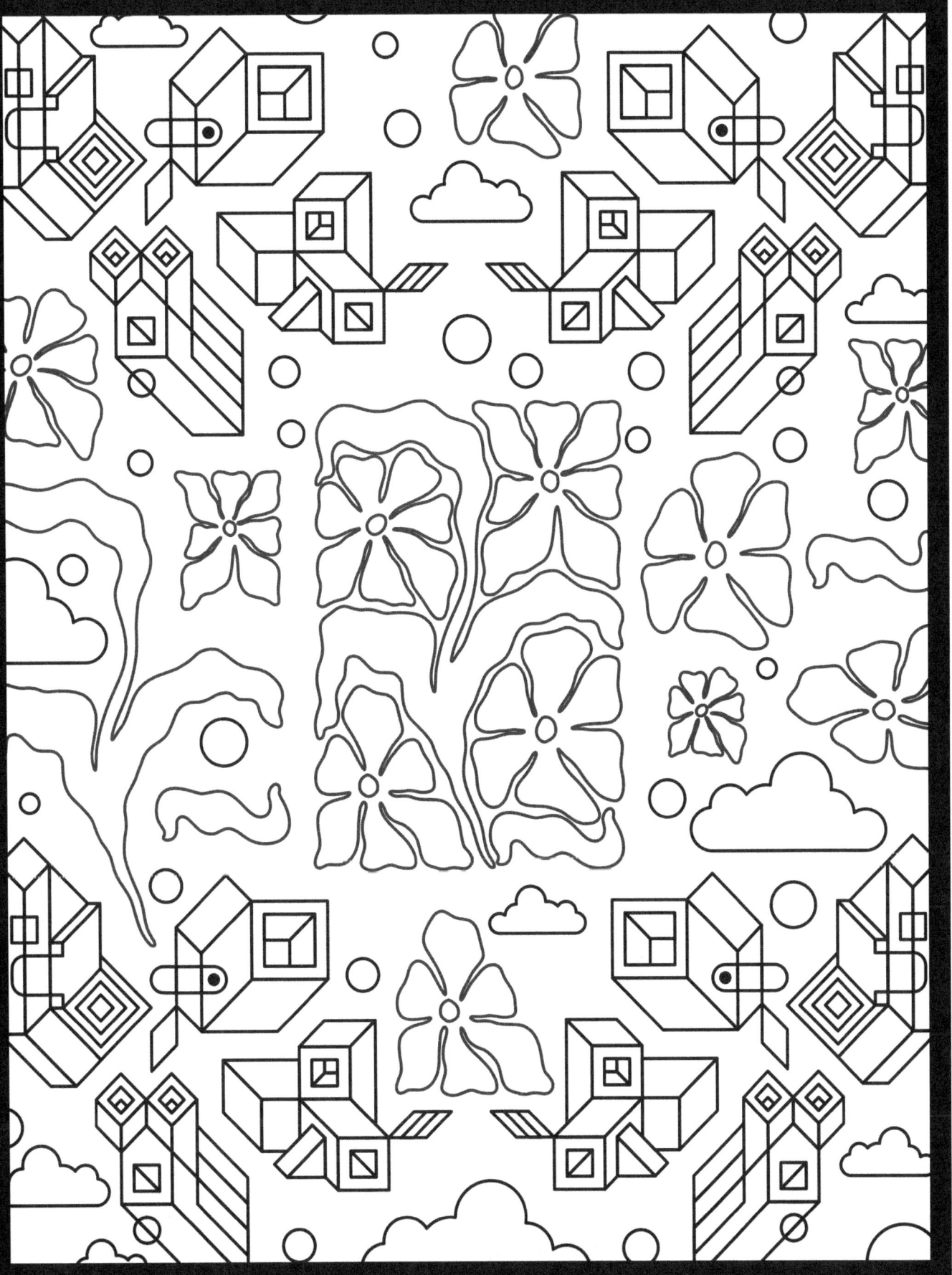

AGAIN AND AGAIN

LIFE GOES ON

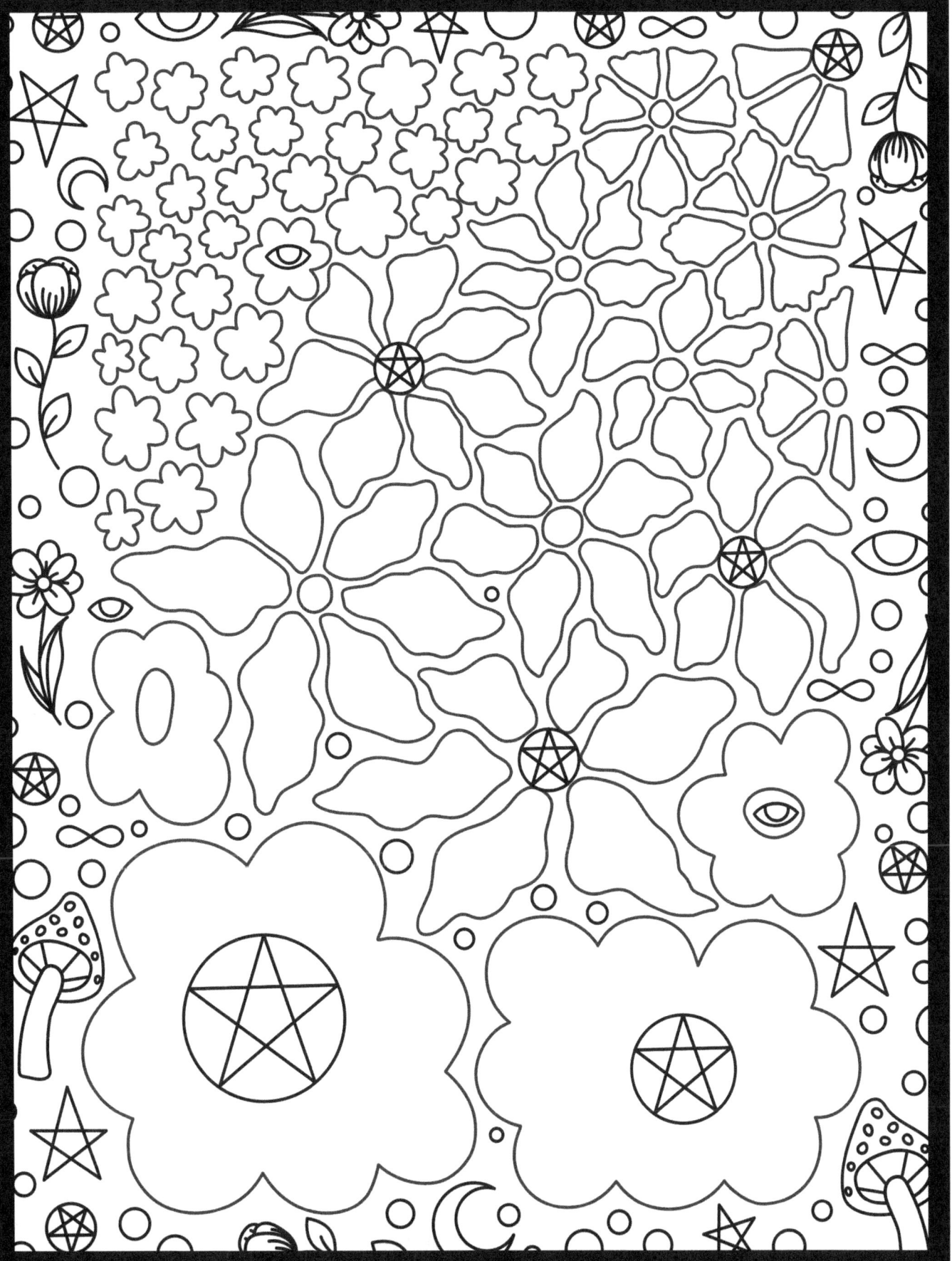

LIFE FINDS A WAY

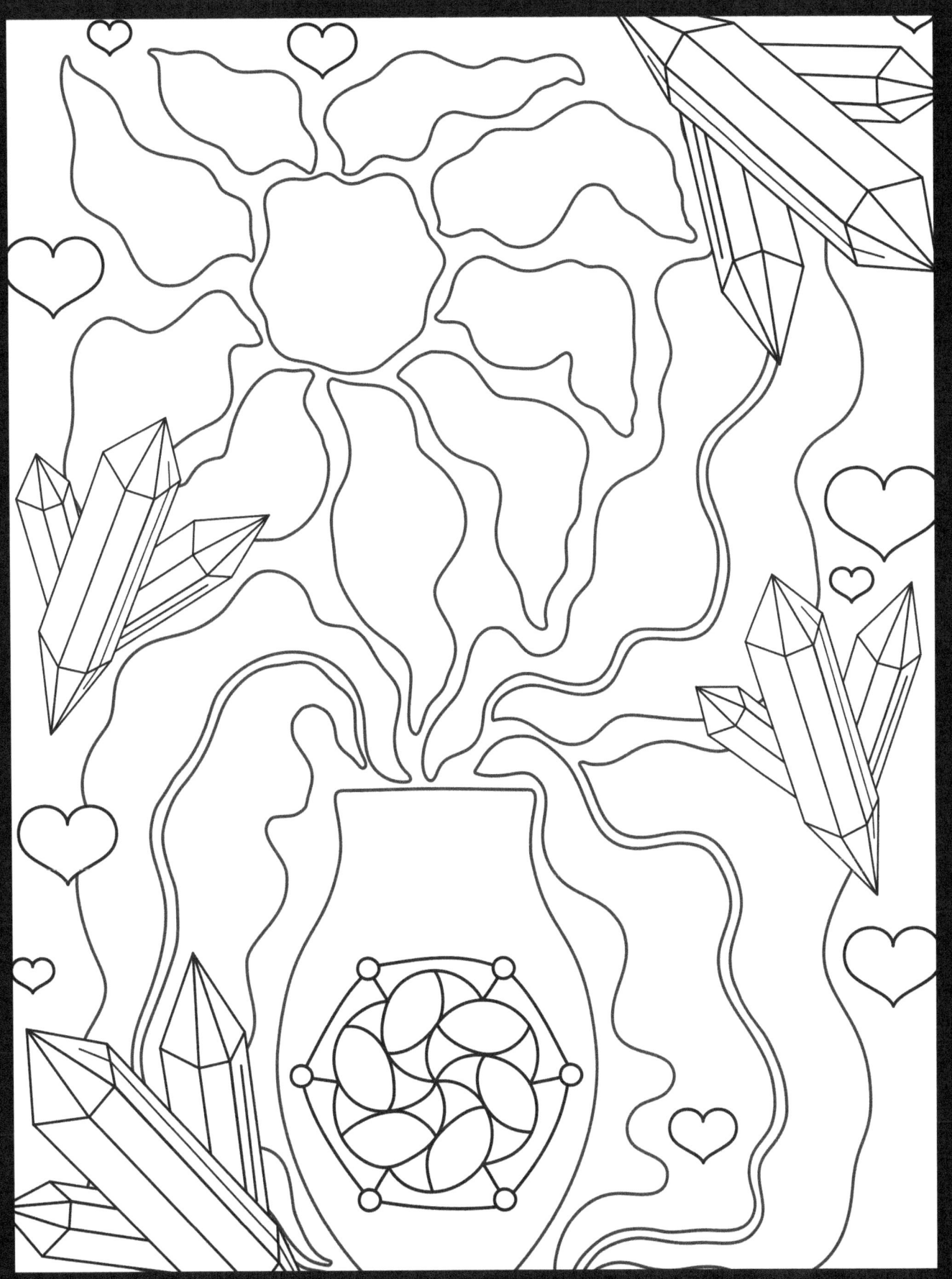

ENERGY WORK

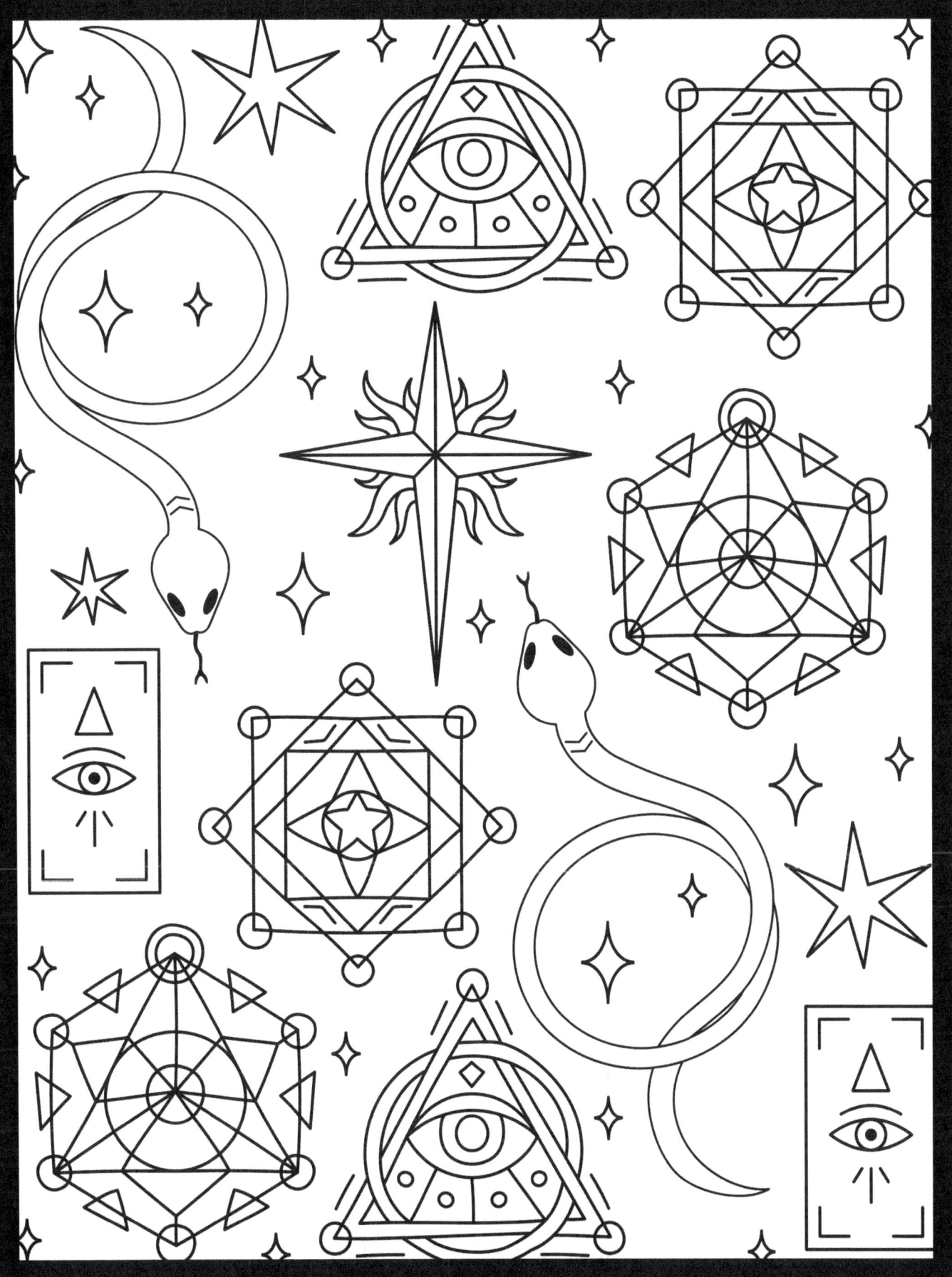

SLITHERING SNAKES

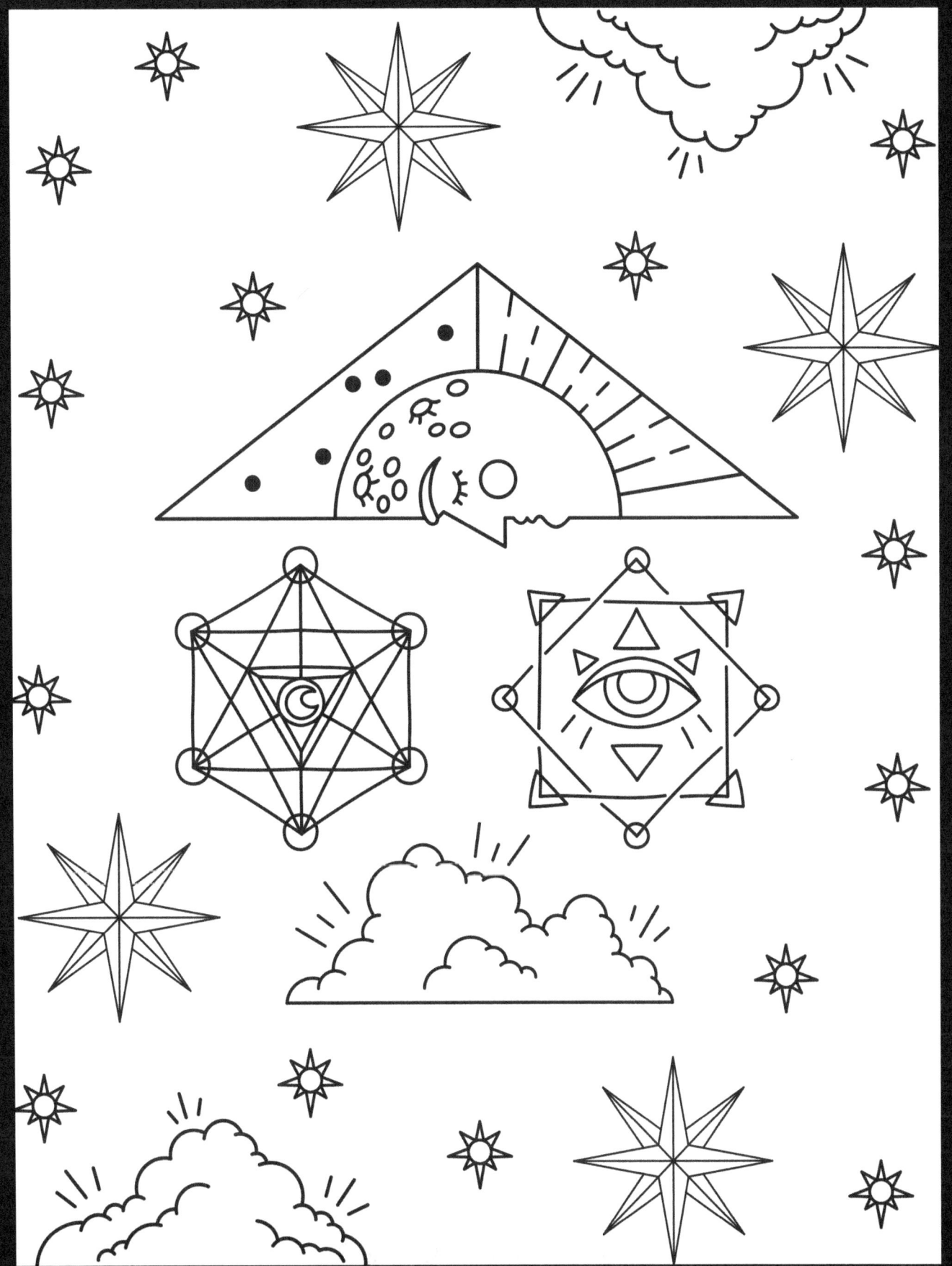

SYMBOLS IN THE MIDDLE

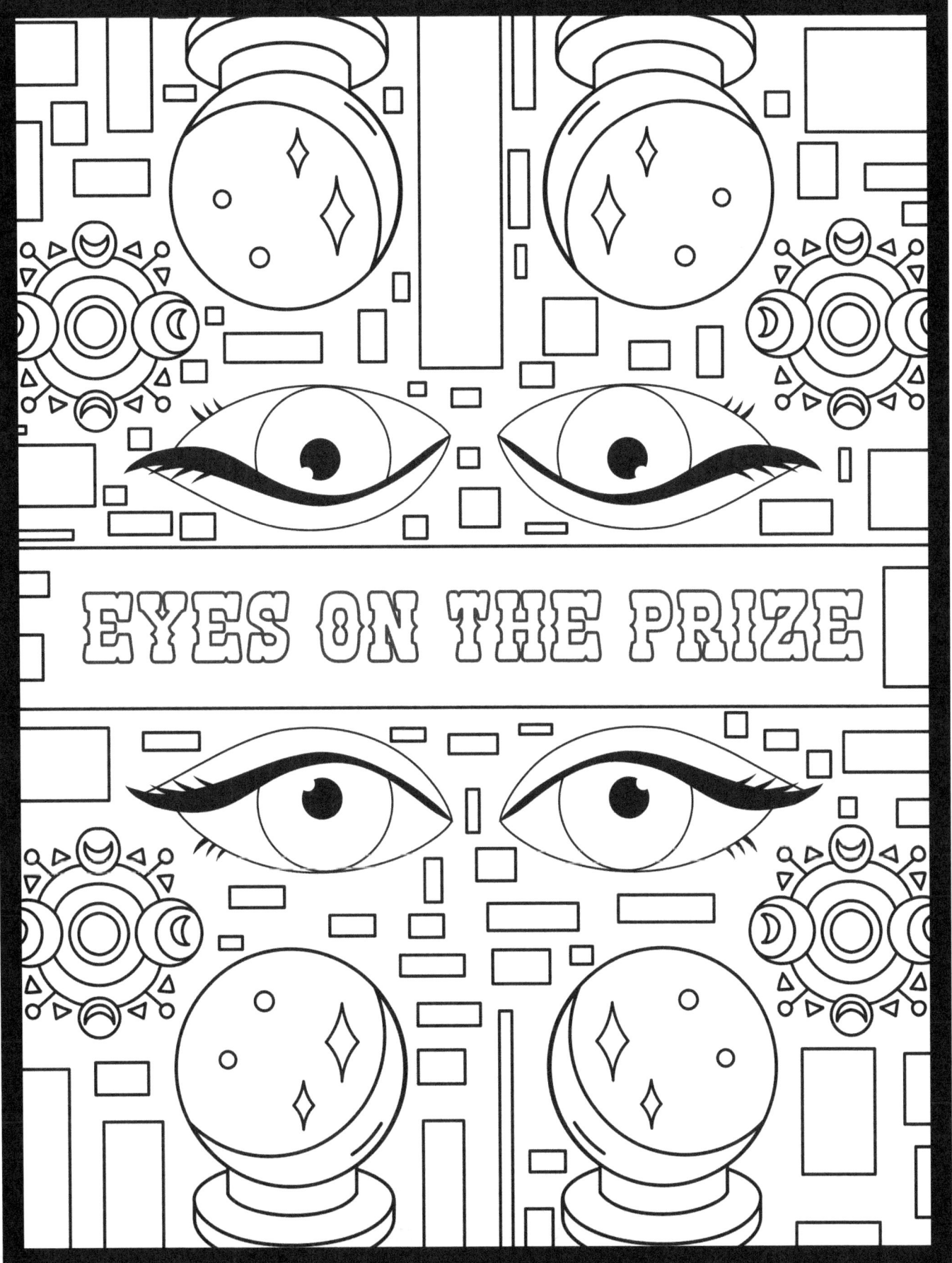

KEEP GOING

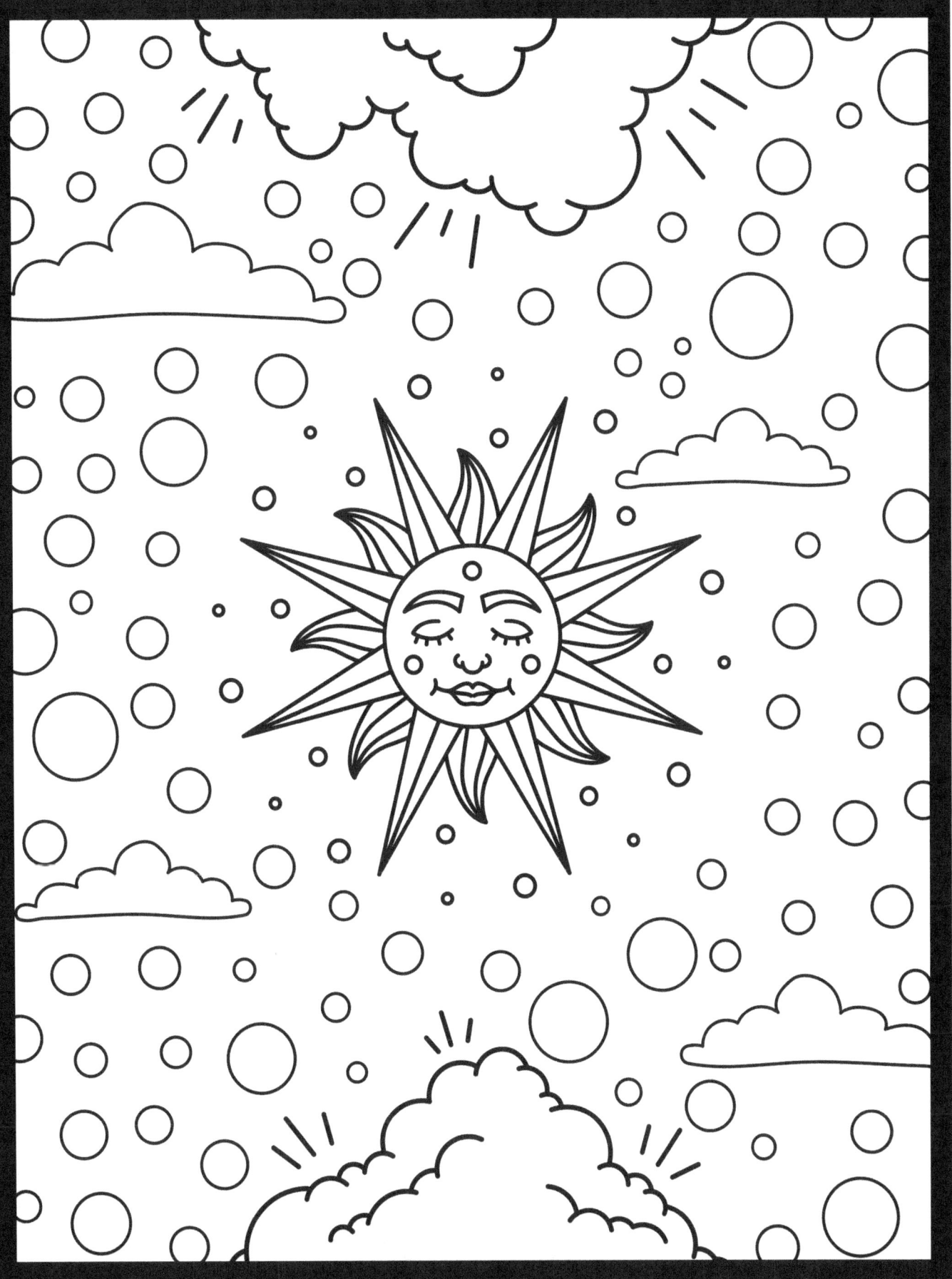

THE SUN WILL SHINE

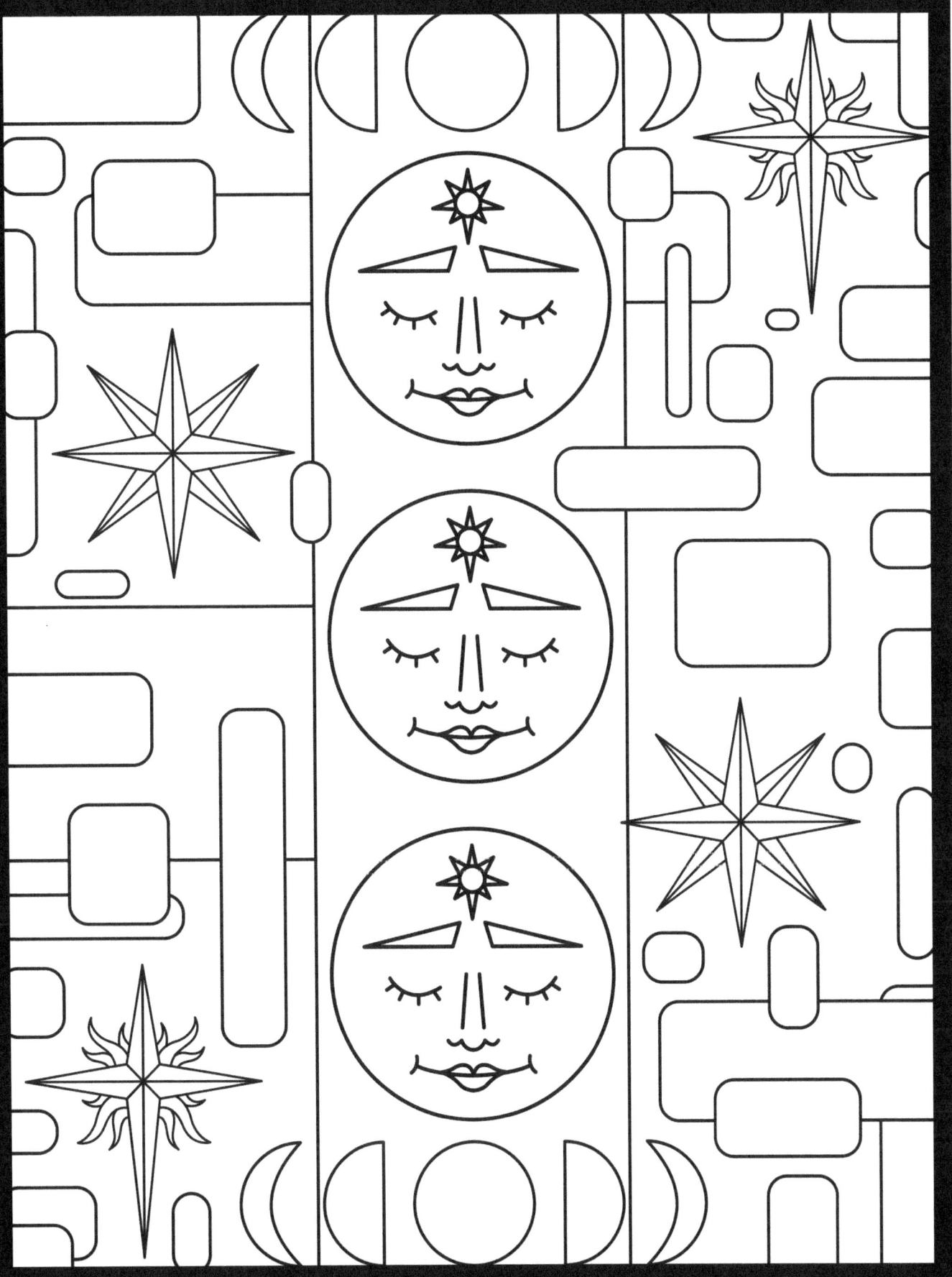

NIGHT WILL COME

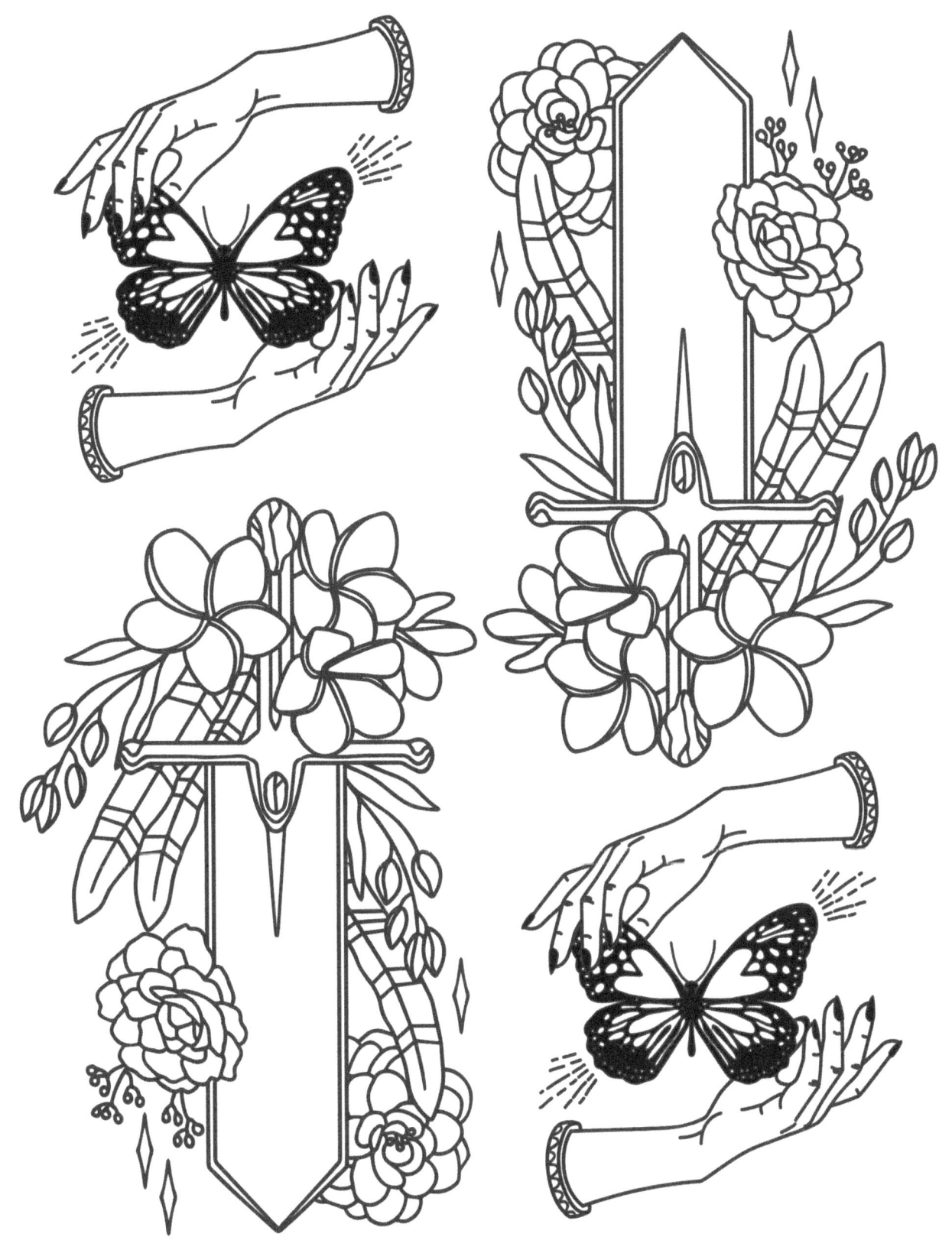

STAY SHARP

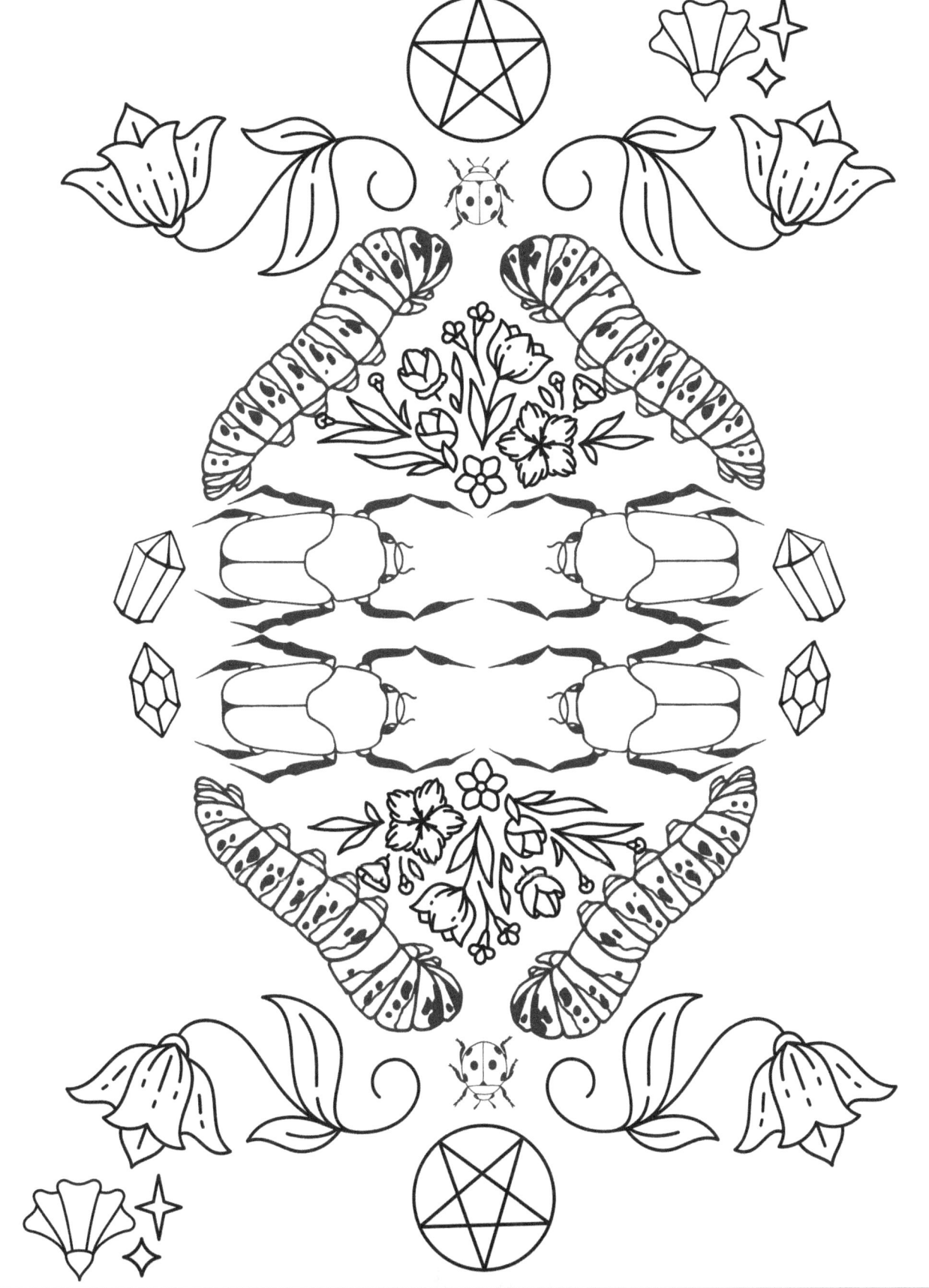

SACRED SHAPES

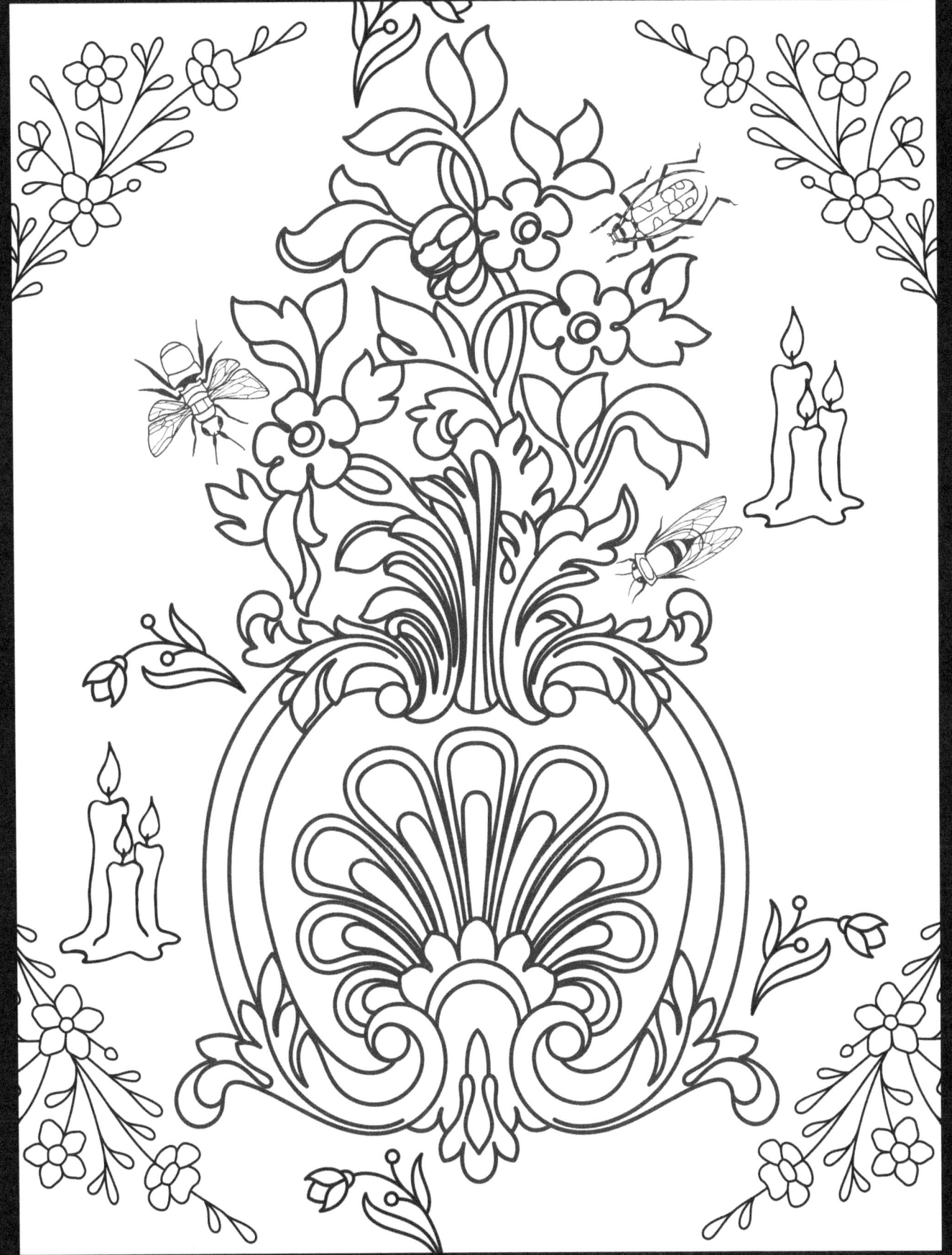

PURPOSE

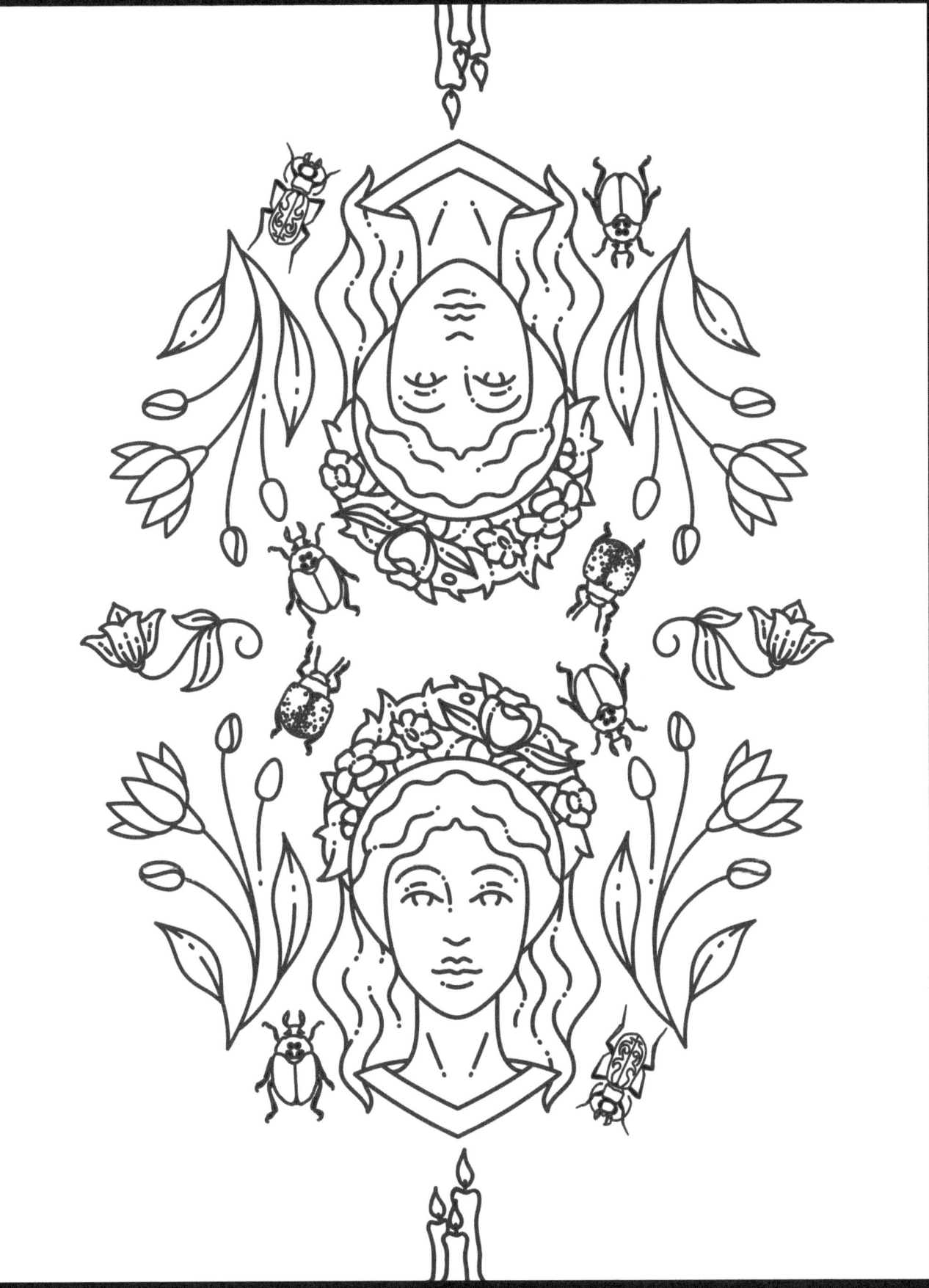

GODDESS LIGHT

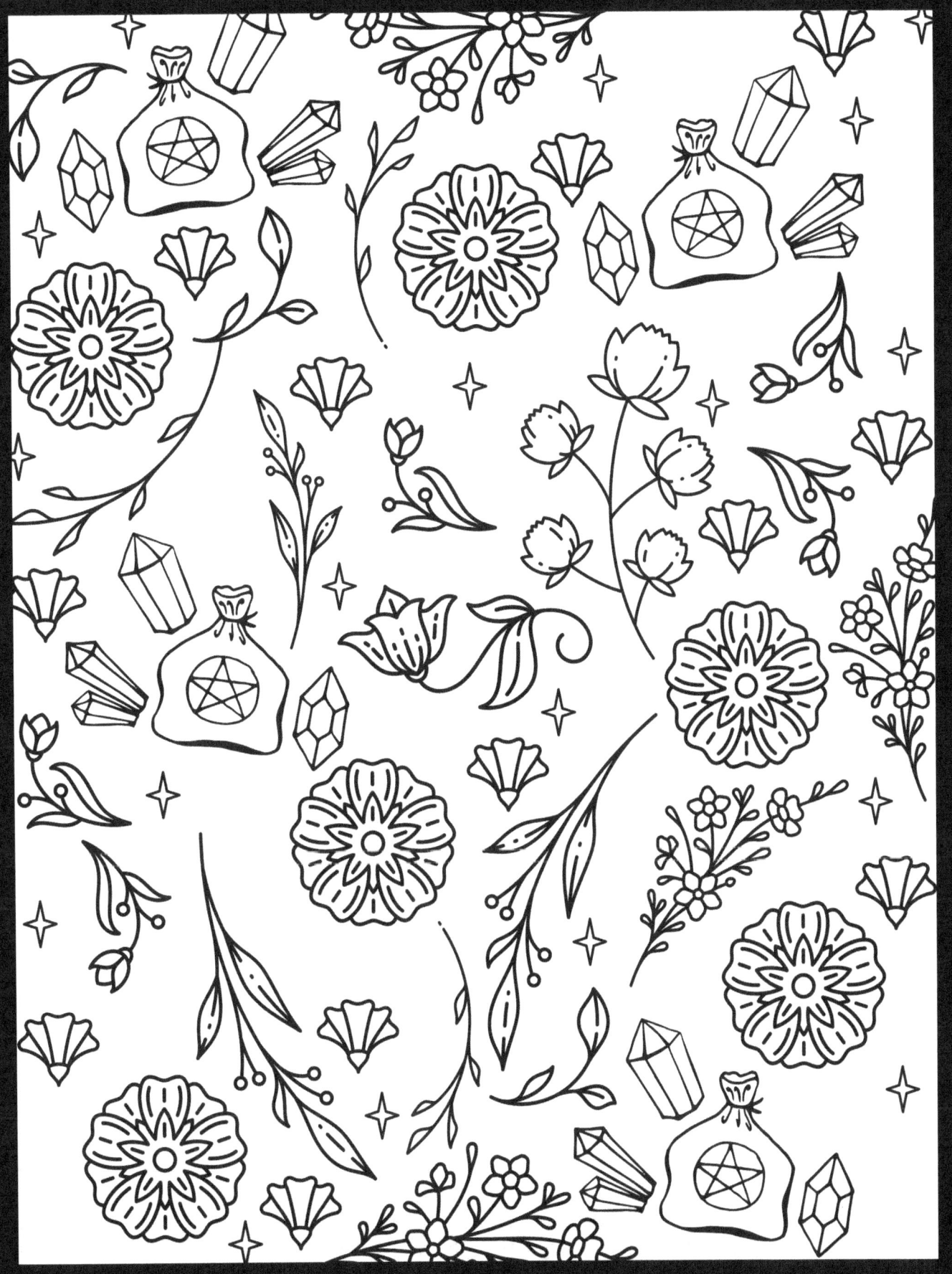

TREASURES BEYOND MEASURES

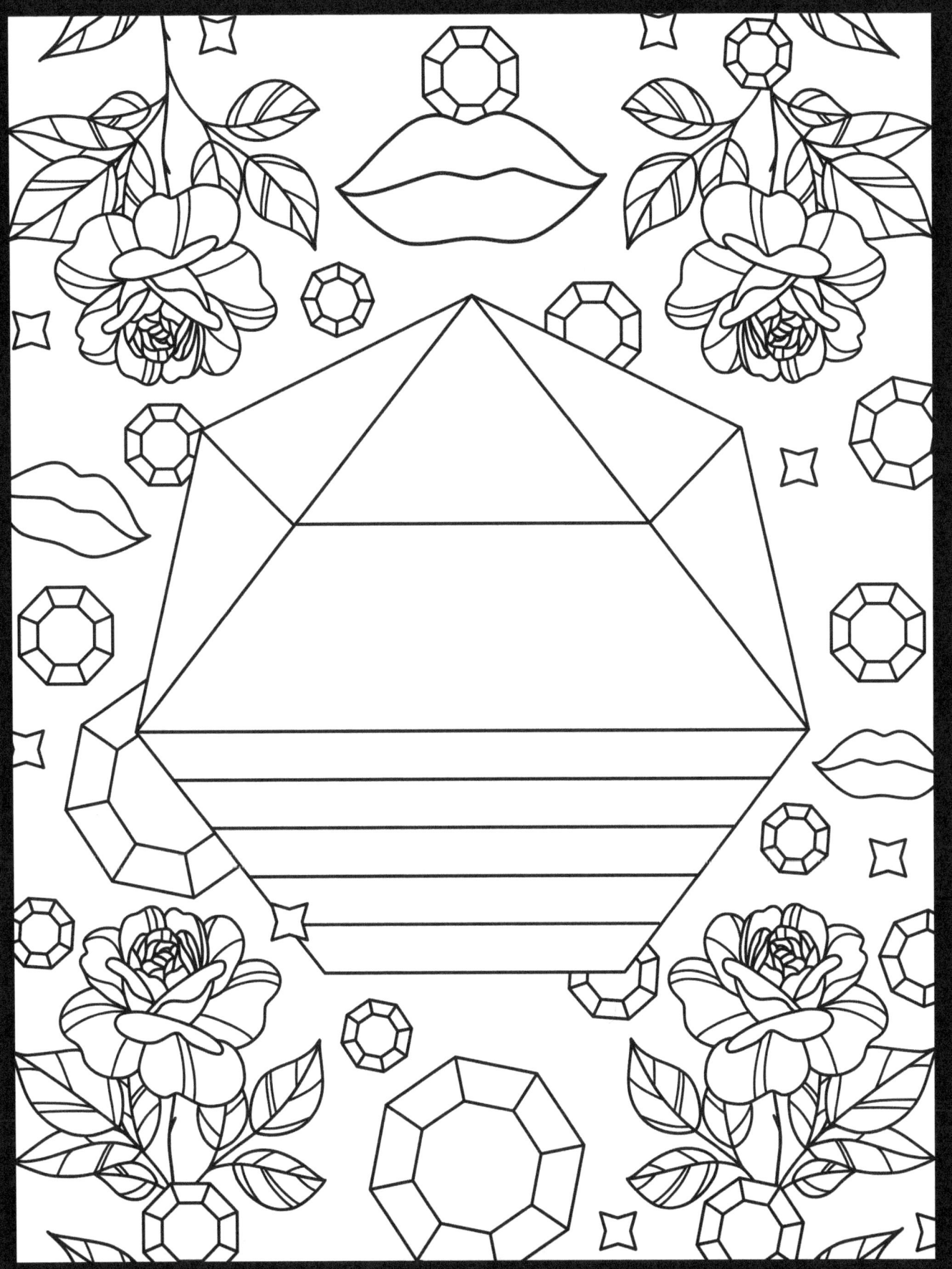

NATURALLY

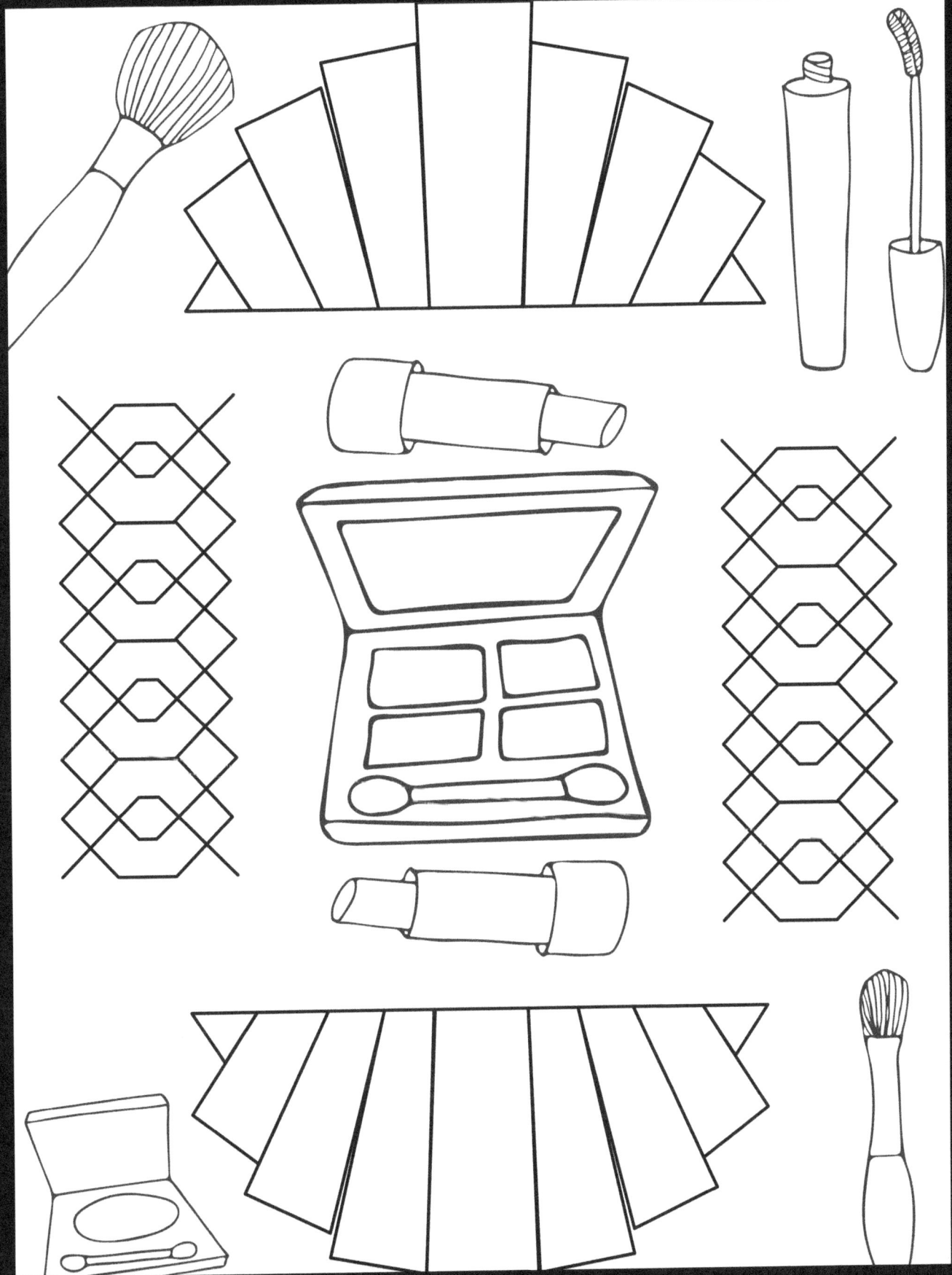

STAY BEAUTIFUL